Mrs Findlay's
Broadwood Square Piano

Michael Hannon

Michael Hannon

with CD recordings by Inja Davidović

First published in Sheffield, United Kingdom, in 2015.

ISBN : 978-0-9931814-1-2

A CIP catalogue record for this book is available from the British Library.

Distributed by Ranmoor Publications, Sheffield, S10 3HB. United Kingdom.

info@ranmoorpublications.co.uk

Visit: www.mrsfindlaysbroadwoodsquarepiano.co.uk

Designed, printed and published by Northend Creative Print Solutions, Sheffield. S8 0TZ.

www.northend.co.uk

Contents

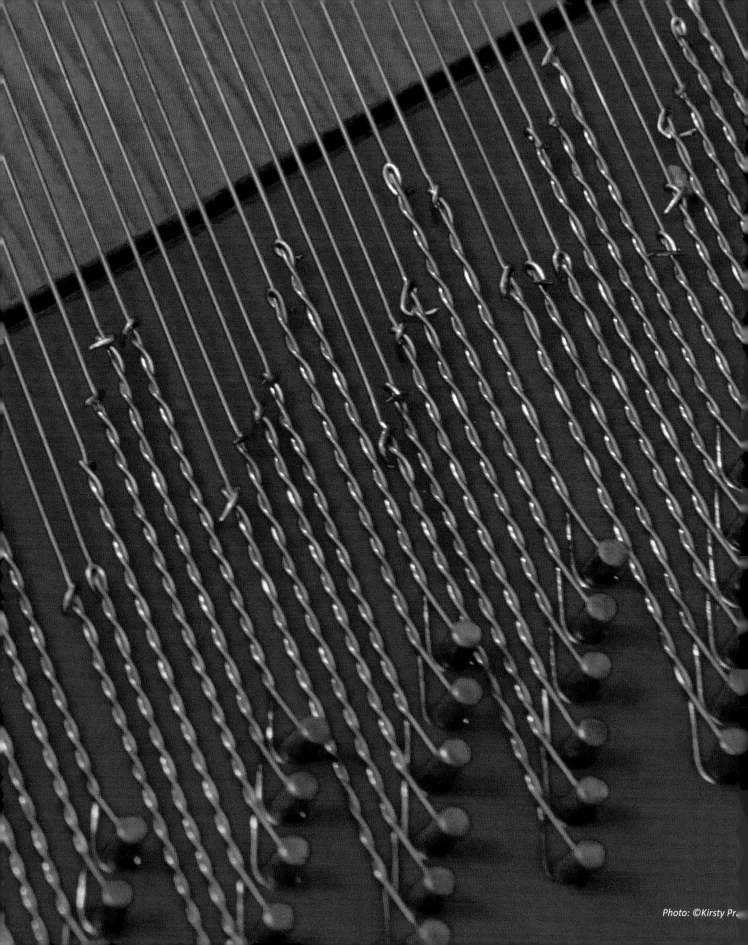

Foreword

by Bill Findlay

*Great, great, great-grandson of Mrs Dorothy Findlay, who bought
the Broadwood square piano new in 1804*

In early 2010, quite out of the blue, I received a remarkable letter from Michael Hannon, author of this book. His enquiry had been passed to me by my late brother Robert who, following illness, had asked me to take over the role of family historian. It was a delightful surprise to learn that the 1804 Broadwood square piano which Michael Hannon's mother Hilda (née Denny) had bought on a whim at a country auction in Ireland in 1977, was the very instrument that my great, great, great-grandmother Dorothy Findlay had bought from Broadwoods in August 1804. Widow of the Glasgow tobacco merchant Robert Findlay, she had been staying in London with their eldest daughter Janet, who was expecting her first baby, and had ordered the piano 'on hire or purchase' from Broadwoods during her visit.

The romantic story of how Mrs Findlay's youngest daughter, 'the Flighty Dorothea', ran off to marry her piano teacher John Donaldson, has been well known in our Findlay family history for generations. And now Inja Davidović's superb recordings on the square piano bring fresh life to this romantic story, evoking their blossoming relationship over the keys of the new instrument some 210 years ago.

Equally extraordinary are the uncanny links that have come to light between our Findlay family and the author's forebears, the Dennys of Dumbarton, with their great shipbuilding tradition. Perhaps the most remarkable of these links was the entrepreneurial joint venture between our two great-grandfathers, TD Findlay and Peter Denny, in establishing the famous 'Irrawaddy Flotilla', immortalized by Kipling in 'The Road to Mandalay, *where the old flotilla lay'*. More recently, it was also such a strange and heart-warming coincidence that my wife Delia and I had bought our house 'Auchenlinnhe' from our old friend Edward Denny, Michael Hannon's late uncle.

It is a great pleasure to write a Foreword to such a fascinating book. Together with my sister-in-law Liisa Findlay, we have been looking forward to its publication with great anticipation.

Bill Findlay

Auchenlinnhe, December 2014

Introduction

In 1977 my mother, Hilda Hannon, bought what was listed as a Broadwood 'spinet' at an auction in Ballycastle, Co Antrim, where she and my father lived in retirement. Although the instrument was in poor condition it was structurally sound and most of its working parts were still in place. Having bought it on a whim, my mother gave it to me, suggesting that I might try restoring it.

The instrument turned out to be a Broadwood 'square piano', dated 1804, serial number 8119. Square pianos, also known as 'box' or 'table' pianos, made their first appearance in England in the 1760s. They were actually oblong in shape, smaller and lighter than the early 'grand' pianos which had been developed from the harpsichord, and rested on a light demountable frame or on removable legs at the corners. They were simpler, cheaper and easier to make than grand pianos and their clear, sweet 'singing' tone and delicate touch had a special appeal. Very soon they became the fashionable instrument of choice, not only for the aristocracy and the wealthy but also the emerging middle classes who, able to afford them, gave them pride of place in their parlours.

The London-based harpsichord and piano maker, John Broadwood, recognized the potential of this new market and developed it into a hugely profitable business. Broadwoods continued to make square pianos until the 1860s when they were overtaken by what we know generically as 'upright' pianos, which had longer keyboards, produced greater resonance and enabled increased volume.

There are still thousands of square pianos in existence around the world, some in fine playable condition, others in distress awaiting restoration. Many others, with their keyboards and actions removed, have been made into dressing tables, writing desks or sideboards. Restoration of period instruments requires not only a high degree of technical skill but also detailed knowledge of the original materials and methods used in their construction. Above all, these early instruments must be treated sympathetically and not over-restored. I therefore decided it would be wiser not to attempt restoration myself but to have the square piano professionally restored to full playing condition.

Eager to find out who the original owner of the instrument might have been, I wrote to Broadwoods in 1980. Apart from confirming that the date 1804 on the name board matched the serial number, they were unable to help as, in their words, 'the records do not exist'. However, almost twenty years later I discovered that the records for my piano *did* in fact exist but had not been catalogued at the time of my initial enquiry. In Michael Cole's definitive book *Broadwood Square Pianos,* published in 2005, he makes frequent reference to the 'porters' books' in the Broadwood archives: these recorded the serial numbers of every instrument leaving or entering the Broadwood works in Great Pulteney Street in London. The archives had been rescued from the former home of the late Captain Evelyn Broadwood, a previous chairman. Conserved and catalogued, they were now available for consultation in the Surrey History Centre in Woking.

The porters' book for 1804 recorded that on Tuesday 10th July Broadwoods delivered the piano 'on hire or purchase' to a Mrs Findlay who was staying with a Mrs Bannatine at 8 New Broad Street in the City of London. After a month's trial Mrs Findlay decided to buy it and have it delivered to her house in Miller Street in Glasgow. Broadwoods collected it on 10th August for repacking and took it to the sailing ship *Eliza* at the Glasgow Wharf on the Thames; Captain Alexander Wilson, her Master and owner, would deliver the piano to Glasgow by sea.

The challenge now was to find out who this Mrs Findlay was, why she was staying with Mrs Bannatine in London, and who would be playing the new piano in Glasgow. What turned into a fascinating detective story revealed an extraordinarily romantic but tragic family saga arising directly from Mrs Findlay's youngest daughter Dorothea's piano lessons with her teacher and future husband, John Donaldson. He was to launch a bitter, fruitless legal dispute against the wealthy Findlay family that lasted almost half a century. The story also revealed several uncanny coincidences in the 19th and 20th centuries between Mrs Findlay's Scottish descendents and my mother's forebears in the Denny shipbuilding family in Dumbarton.

There is no documentary evidence of what happened to the piano itself between its delivery to Mrs Findlay's Glasgow house in 1804 and an auction in Belfast in 1949. That gap may never be filled, but between those dates the dramatic saga of 'the Flighty Dorothea' Findlay and John Donaldson, and the extraordinary links between the Findlay and Denny families are so compelling that I decided a book had to be written. Little did my mother imagine what her whimsical purchase of the square piano at a country auction in Ireland would eventually reveal.

Michael Hannon
Sheffield, 2015

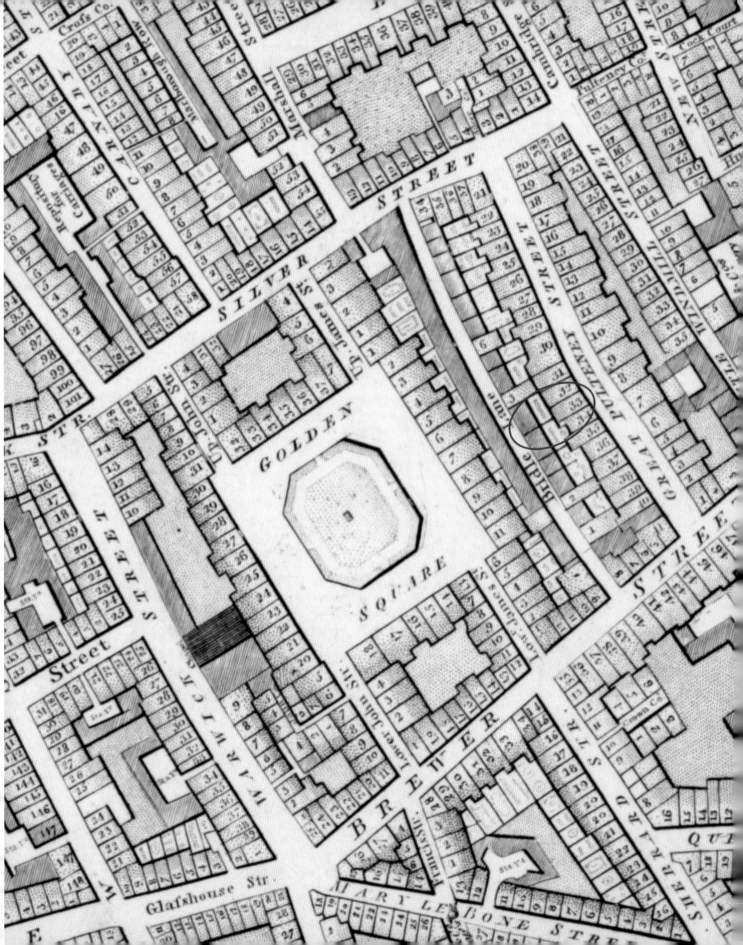

1. New Deliveries

The porters arrive for work

Early on the morning of Tuesday 10th July 1804 two porters turned up for work delivering instruments for the famous London piano-makers John Broadwood and Son. They checked in at the yard in Bridle Lane behind the company's showroom at 33 Great Pulteney Street, near Golden Square. Mr Chandler, the senior of the two, and Mr Clark checked their schedule for the day in the porters' book in the yard office and saw that their first delivery was a square piano, serial number 8069, addressed to a Mr Hughes at a Mr Luckington's residence in Finsbury Square. Another square piano, number 8119, was to be delivered 'on hire or purchase' to a Mrs Findlay who was staying with a Mrs Bannatine at 8 New Broad Street in the City. The entry showed it was a Square Piano Forte [SPF] with additional French frame [addff] and damper pedal [DP].

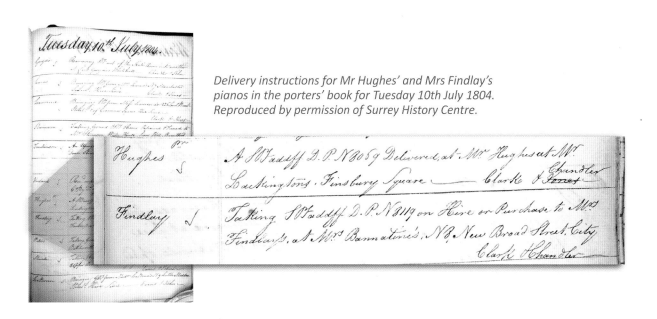

Delivery instructions for Mr Hughes' and Mrs Findlay's pianos in the porters' book for Tuesday 10th July 1804. Reproduced by permission of Surrey History Centre.

Opposite: Broadwoods at 33 Great Pulteney Street, with yard behind in Bridle Lane, from Richard Horwood's 1792 'Plan of the Cities of London & Westminster'. © The British Library Board, Maps 148.e.7.

METEOROLOGICAL TABLE for July, 1804. By W. Cary, Strand.											

William Cary's temperature recordings for 10th July 1804 from The Gentleman's Magazine. Courtesy: National Meteorological Archive.

Planning their day

Mr Chandler knew that Finsbury Square was quite near New Broad Street but thought it wise to check their route first on the office copy of Horwood's *Map of London*. This had been first published in 1792 and, although expensive at the time, Mr John Broadwood ('Mr Broadwood Senior') knew it would be a wise investment. He had ambitious plans for increasing his piano sales across the capital.

Another porter, Mr Jefford, who was in the office checking the map for his own deliveries, mentioned that he knew Mrs Bannatine's house in New Broad Street, as he had delivered another

As usual at 8.00 o'clock that morning Mr William Cary, an amateur meteorologist living in the Strand, checked the thermometer in his garden and recorded a temperature of 66°F under a cloudy sky. He added this reading to his monthly weather report for publication in the August issue of *The Gentleman's Magazine*. From the overcast sky, it looked as if there could be rain later and that it wouldn't be too hot a day for the horses pulling the Broadwood wagons or the porters doing their heavy lifting.

Entry for Mr Bannatyne's piano in the porters' book for 23rd May 1803. Reproduced by permission of Surrey History Centre.

Opposite: Broadwood's 'Square Yard' in Bridle Lane behind 33 Great Pulteney Street. Reproduced by permission of John Broadwood and Sons Ltd.

'square' there on 23rd May the previous year. He was an old Broadwood hand who enjoyed meeting the company's customers and had a good memory for names. Judging by the delivery date of Mrs Bannatine's instrument, he thought its serial number must have been between 7330 and 7350.

Mr Jefford remembered Mrs Bannatine as a young newly-wed with a refined Scottish accent. He particularly recalled her saying that they had been married in March that year by her clergyman grandfather who was also, he seemed to remember, some sort of professor in Glasgow. He thought the piano might have been a wedding present from her husband as the bill for it had been made out to him.

Loading up and checking out

Expecting rain later, Mr Chandler and Mr Clark loaded the two crates under the tarpaulin covering their wagon and led their well-matched pair of horses towards the gate of the small mews yard on Bridle Lane. There they checked the pianos out, adding a tick opposite each entry in the hefty leather-bound porters' book where all instruments leaving or entering the yard were recorded.

They set off at a steady pace towards Finsbury Square, picking their way carefully through the busy traffic. At Mr Luckington's house they were told to leave Mr Hughes' piano in the stable still safely packed in its crate. Mr Hughes, who had ordered it, was abroad at the time; on his return he would have it sent to his country house.

Resting the horses

At midday over in the Strand, Mr Cary's diligent thermometer was now registering 60°F. With time to spare and the day getting a little colder, the porters stopped to let the horses drink from a trough in the Square. They sat under a tree enjoying the bread and cheese their wives had prepared for them early that morning. They shared fatherly concerns about their sons, one in the Royal Navy fighting the Spaniards, the other in the Army fighting the French. They wondered if this warring would ever stop: perhaps the young William Pitt, who had just been appointed Prime Minister for the second time at the age of only 35, could put an end to it and bring their sons safely home again. They also discussed the latest gossip about King George III, who had been on the throne for forty-four years now. He was rumoured to be unwell again, suffering from a strange disease; some folk thought he was losing his mind. Perhaps they could pick up more news when they next delivered a Broadwood instrument to Windsor Castle.

Mrs Findlay comes to the door

After resting the horses, they drove the short distance to New Broad Street. The numbering of the houses was not straightforward but having eventually found number 8, Mr Chandler used the highly polished brass knocker to announce their arrival. A manservant answered the door and asked them to wait until his mistress was ready to receive them. Several minutes later an older woman, who sounded Scottish, appeared at the door. She explained that she was the Mrs Findlay who had ordered the piano on hire or purchase.

Mrs Findlay asked them to carry the piano in as quietly as possible as her daughter Janet, the mistress of the house, was expecting a baby within the next few weeks and having a rest. They carried the crate up the steps, through the front door under the elegant fanlight and gently set it down in the hall. The horses waited patiently in the street as the clouds gathered and the rain began to fall.

When she signed for the piano in the Broadwood receipt book, Mrs Findlay noticed that her daughter's married surname 'Bannatyne' was incorrectly spelt as 'Bannatine'. She pointed this out to Mr Chandler who assured her he would ask the chief clerk to correct it in his ledgers.

The Broadwood porters deliver Mrs Findlay's piano to 8 New Broad Street.
Drawing by Kate Pickering.

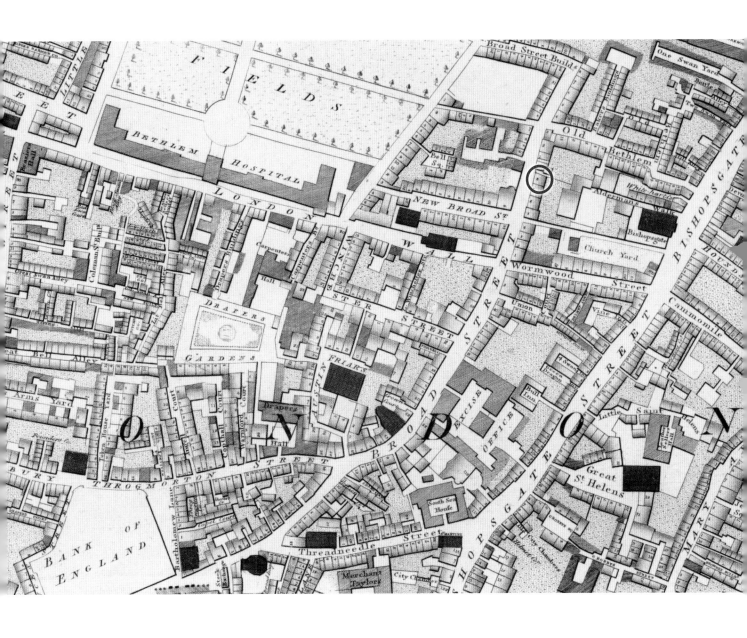

*8 New Broad Street, London Wall, Throgmorton Street
and The Bank of England. From Richard Horwood's
1792 'Plan of the Cities of London & Westminster'.
© The British Library Board, Maps 148.e.7.*

Left: Swivelling brass medallion covering the end of an underframe bolt.
Photo: © 2014 Kirsty Prince.
Below: Optional damper pedal attached to the damper rail with a thin wire.
Photo: © 2014 Kirsty Prince.
Bottom: Mrs Findlay's square piano, lids closed, sitting on its 'French' underframe with the music shelf and pedal below.

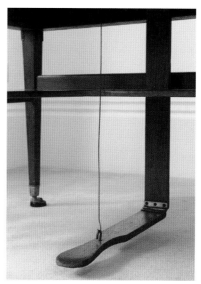

Setting up the piano

Removing the lid from the crate, the porters took out what the Broadwood catalogue had described as the 'French' underframe which was packed on top in its component parts. They bolted its 'stretchers', or cross-members, to the delicately tapered gate-leg ends, ensuring that the swivelling brass medallions covered the heads of the heavy bolts that held the frame together.

They added the music shelf below. The underframe was very light and easy to move into the parlour where Mr Jefford had delivered Janet Bannatyne's Broadwood the year before. They carried in the heavy instrument and carefully lowered it on to the underframe, taking care not to get their fingers trapped between the two. Beneath the underframe they attached the damper [i.e. sustaining] pedal offered as an optional extra for square pianos. They checked that the lid, with its slender stays, and the folding music stand were all well fitted and in good working order.

A matching pair of Broadwoods

The two highly polished pianos sat side by side in the parlour. The cartouches on the name boards above the ivory and ebony keys were beautifully veneered in fiddle-back sycamore. Finely written in Indian ink, the inscriptions read: *John Broadwood and Son, Makers to His Majesty and the Princesses, Great Pulteney Street, Golden Square, London,* with their respective dates above. Mr Chandler surreptitiously checked the serial number at the back of Janet Bannatyne's 1803 instrument and saw that it was 7339, so Mr Jefford's memory for serial numbers had been as sharp as ever.

Cartouche on Mrs Findlay's piano, reading: '1804, John Broadwood and Son, Makers to His Majesty and the Princesses, Great Pulteney Street, Golden Square, London'.

A word of advice

Mr Chandler ran his calloused fingers up and down the keys of the new piano. He wasn't a piano tuner but, as the senior man, it was his responsibility to check that the action and pedal were working properly. While giving the keys a final clean and polish, he advised Mrs Findlay to keep the pianos out of direct sunlight but always to leave the keyboard lids open to prevent the ivory keys turning yellow. One of the Broadwood tuners would call within a few days once Mrs Findlay's piano had become acclimatized to its new location. He would tune the other one too if she wished, so that they could happily be played together. The first tuning of a new piano was free; subsequent tunings would cost four shillings each. Wishing Mrs Findlay well for the safe arrival of her daughter's baby, the porters drove back to the yard in Bridle Lane.

A new grandchild

A week later on Tuesday 17th July 1804, a little earlier than her mother had expected for a first pregnancy, Janet Bannatyne safely delivered a baby girl, Mrs Findlay's first grandchild. With the excitement of the new arrival and sleepless nights, there wasn't much opportunity for mother and daughter to compare the two instruments but one afternoon, when the baby had finally fallen asleep, they managed to play a few pieces comparing the two newly tuned pianos.

Mrs Findlay makes a decision

Mrs Findlay specially liked the new square piano's sweet tone and delicate touch. She also enjoyed using a damper pedal for the first time: when depressing it with her left foot, the notes continued sounding after she lifted her fingers from the keys. She decided to buy the piano and sent instructions to Broadwoods to collect and forward it to her Glasgow home in Miller Street, where her two younger daughters, Annabella and Dorothea, would enjoy playing it. Her son Robert, perhaps not the most musical member of the family, might allow himself to try it too. She planned to return to Glasgow by coach before the piano was finally delivered after its journey by sea from London. She wanted to see the excitement on her daughters' faces when it arrived at the door.

The christening

Three weeks later, on the morning of Friday 10th August, John and Janet Bannatyne's baby daughter was christened 'Dorothea' in the Scotch Church on London Wall, at the southwest corner of Finsbury Circus. The Kirk, as they knew it, was within easy walking distance of New Broad Street.

Mrs Findlay was very pleased at their choice of the name Dorothea. It was the same as her youngest daughter's name and very close to her own baptismal name 'Dorretty', both meaning 'Gift of God'. When she became an adult, however, Mrs Findlay preferred to be called 'Dorothy'.

*Above: Mrs Findlay's square piano as delivered to
8 New Broad Street on 10th July 1804.*

Mrs Findlay found it hard to conceal her inner sadness that her late husband Robert was not there to see their first grandchild christened. He had been killed in a riding accident just two years previously, so hadn't even lived to give Janet away at her wedding back home in Glasgow.

Broadwoods collect the piano

Later that afternoon, when the Minister of the Scotch Church and other Scottish friends joined the family 'to wet the bairn's head', another Broadwood porter, Mr Evans, arrived unexpectedly to collect Mrs Findlay's piano. He took it straight back to the Broadwood works where it was to be prepared for its journey to Glasgow.

A trip to the bank

On Saturday mornings Mrs Findlay's son-in-law, John Bannatyne, usually walked the short distance to his office in Throgmorton Street near the Bank of England. He and his late father-in-law, Robert Findlay, had been partners in the successful trading firm of 'Findlay, Bannatyne & Co' which had extensive business interests in Europe, across the Atlantic and, not least, in the City of London where the company was listed among the 'Members of the Society' at Lloyd's. During her time in London, Mrs Findlay had much to discuss with him about her husband's estate and his shares in the business as he had died intestate. On this particular Saturday, 11th August, rather than going to his office, John Bannatyne took his mother-in-law to the bank as she needed to pay cash for the piano but was anxious about carrying a large sum of money around the London streets on her own.

Mrs Findlay pays the bill

John Bannatyne's carriage took them straight from the bank to the Broadwood showrooms at 33 Great Pulteney Street. Mr Broadwood Senior, now 72 and semi-retired, was spending more time with his family in his smart Kensington Gore residence so it was his son, James Shudi Broadwood, who received them. He was now running the company's everyday business and made it a priority to meet his wealthier customers, especially those with connections in the City. Like his Scottish father, he was keen to continue developing the business north of the border, particularly through their Broadwood agents in Glasgow, a city now enjoying great prosperity as a world centre for tobacco trading.

The fashionably dressed James Broadwood spared no expense entertaining Mrs Findlay and her son-in-law with his most expensive brand of tea and best biscuits. She then paid his chief clerk a total of £33-11s-6d [ca. £2,600 at 2013 prices]. The piano, with its optional extra damper pedal, cost £31-10s-0d. The balance of £2-1s-6d included 18s-0d for the new case, £1-2s-0d for a new leather cover, and 1s-6d for 'cartage' and 'wharfage'. To her son-in-law's embarrassment, Mrs Findlay castigated the chief clerk for misspelling her daughter's married name. He assured her that any 'Bannatine' ledger entries would be corrected; not all of them ever were.

Entrance to John Broadwood & Sons, 33 Great Pulteney Street.
Reproduced by permission of John Broadwood & Sons Ltd.

James Shudi Broadwood (1772-1851). Watercolour ca.1820; artist unknown.
Reproduced by permission of John Broadwood & Sons Ltd.

Broadwood ledger entry for 11th August 1804: Mrs Findlay pays £33-11s-6d in cash.
Reproduced by permission of Surrey History Centre.

Delivery to the Glasgow Wharf

Early the following week, Mr Evans took the piano from the Broadwood yard across London to the Glasgow Wharf on the north bank of the River Thames, a little down-river from the Tower of London. The porters' book said it was to go to Captain Alexander Wilson on board the sailing ship *Eliza* for eventual delivery to Glasgow, addressed to Mrs Findlay's house in Miller Street - but no house number was given.

Mrs Findlay returns to Glasgow

Mrs Findlay returned to Glasgow by coach. Although sad to be leaving her daughter and new grandchild, she was happy that they were both in good health and confident that they would continue to flourish. She was also very pleased with her new purchase and wondered what part it might play in Annabella and Dorothea's musical and social life in Glasgow in the years ahead.

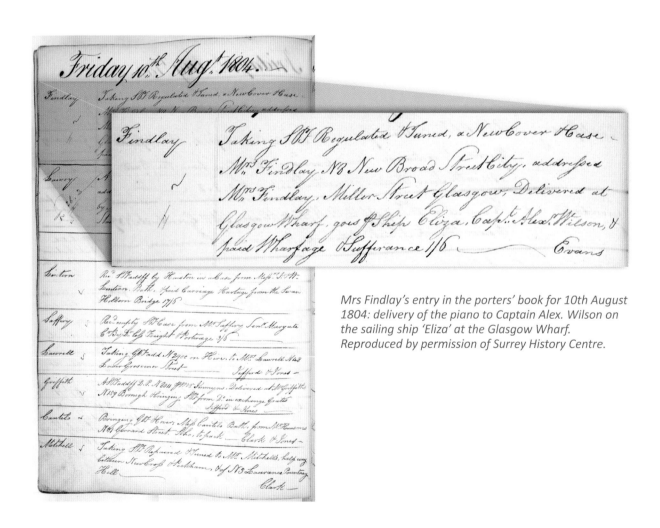

Mrs Findlay's entry in the porters' book for 10th August 1804: delivery of the piano to Captain Alex. Wilson on the sailing ship 'Eliza' at the Glasgow Wharf. Reproduced by permission of Surrey History Centre.

2. The Sloop 'Eliza'

Broadwoods pack up the piano

On Monday 13th August 1804, Mrs Findlay's square piano had been thoroughly checked and its action regulated in the Broadwood workshop. The carpenters wrapped it in a new leather cloth for protection and carefully packed it into one of the specially lined waterproof crates used for transporting instruments by sea. The next morning, with the help of another porter in the yard, Mr Evans loaded the heavy crate on to his wagon and drove it to the Glasgow Wharf.

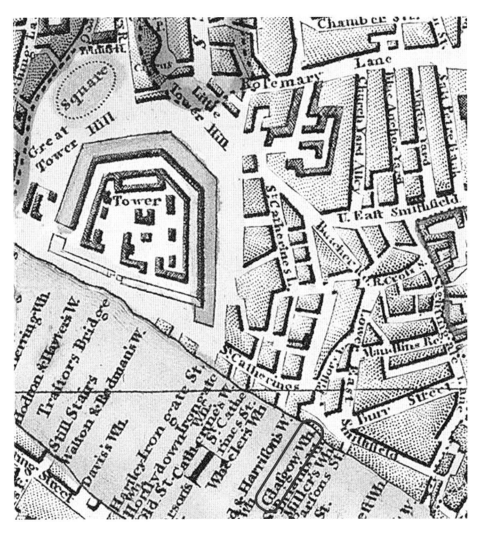

From Fairbairn's 1802 Map of London, showing the Glasgow Wharf in the bottom right hand corner, down-river from the Tower, opposite Burr Street. Reproduced by permission of Motco Enterprises Limited (www.motco.com).

Painting of the Humber sloop 'Harry' by Reuben Chappell. The 'Harry' was similar in dimension, tonnage and rig to Captain Wilson's 'Eliza'.
© National Maritime Museum, Greenwich, London. Reproduced with kind permission of the artist's estate.

Delivery to the 'Eliza'

At the wharf entrance, he paid the gateman the 1s-6d for 'wharfage' and 'suffrance', i.e. harbour dues and insurance. The *Eliza* was tied up alongside the wharf where her crew were busily sorting out cargo for stowage below. Captain Alexander Wilson, her Master and owner, signed for the piano and instructed two crew members to lift the heavy crate across the gangplank. Carrying it carefully down the companionway, they stowed it below the single deck, lashing it securely alongside the mast. Captain Wilson was determined to sail on the turn of the tide at 6.46 on the Wednesday morning.

'A1 at Lloyd's'

At her survey in Leith in 1799 the *Eliza* had been rated 'A1 at Lloyd's', the 'A' signifying a vessel of the 'First Class', the '1' a vessel built of 'First Quality' materials. Captain Wilson had had her built in 1796 as a single-decker sloop, drawing only eight feet of water when laden to her 71-ton capacity. He had taken careful account of the fact that the Forth & Clyde Canal had been opened to its full length from Grangemouth on the Firth of Forth to Port Dundas in Glasgow in 1790.

1 —	Sr	Warthen	113	Spain		Capt.	10	Lo.Diepp	E 1 0½
2 —	Bg	Wronghm	141	Bonefs	7	Webfter	11	Lh	A 1 3 s D
3 —Sw s.W&C	P. Wilder	253	Spain	12	Alexander	14	Lo.Chrlft.	E 1 0½ s D R
4 —	Sp	A. Wilfon	71	Scotl'd	8	Capt.	9	LhBonefs	A 1 01 s D
5 —	S s	Wafhe	140	N Brnf.	17	Antigua	11	Du.	l. 2 99 s D W
6 —&Ann S s.W&C 02	J. Parfons	459	E.Indie BB.Drp. 98	9	Lenox&C.	18	Lo. India	A 1 98
7 —	Bg	R. Rice	87	Teek Neath	22	Capt.	10	La.Coaftr	E 1 0½

The 'Eliza' listed at entry 284 in Lloyd's Register for 1804, showing Captain A. Wilson as her owner. Reproduced by permission of Lloyd's Register Information Centre.

The Forth and Clyde Canal

The new canal had been funded largely by wealthy Glasgow tobacco merchants who needed a swift, reliable transport link 'from-sea-to-sea' for their exports to the main European ports. The first vessel to pass through the canal from West to East had been the sloop *Agnes* 'of 80 tons burthen', drawing eight feet when fully laden. The first to complete the return journey was another sloop, the *Mary McEwen.* Thus a sloop that could do double duty as sea-going vessel and canal transport would be a clever investment. The canal had been designed on the principle of 'clear air draught', that is with opening bridges throughout, so there were no restrictions on headroom. Thus the purpose-built *Eliza* could make the journey all the way from the Thames to the Clyde, either 'tracked' (towed) or sailing through the canal if conditions were favourable.

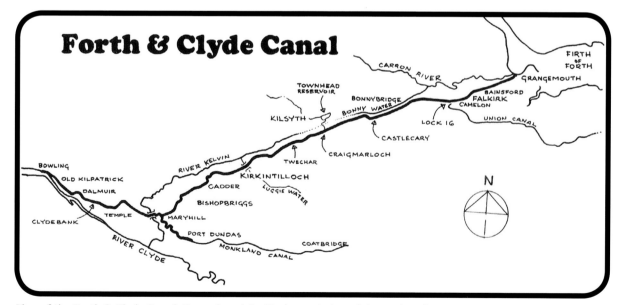

Plan of the Forth & Clyde Canal. Reproduced, by kind permission of the author, from 'A Forth and Clyde Canalbum' by Guthrie Hutton, published in 1991.

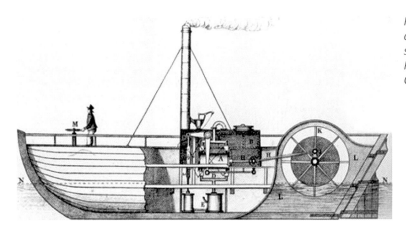

Robert Bowie's 1883 cut-away drawing of the 'Charlotte Dundas', showing her single central paddle wheel.
Public domain image from Wikimedia Commons.

The 'Charlotte Dundas'

Captain Wilson was aware of the trials in March 1802 of William Symington's revolutionary steam-powered tug *Charlotte Dundas,* designed with one large central paddle wheel. She had successfully towed two fully laden 70-ton barges along the canal for 20 miles in six hours, but after the trials her use was banned as there were concerns that her wash would soon erode the canal banks. Captain Wilson did wonder, however, how long it would be before ocean-going vessels like the *Eliza* or larger ones could also be powered by steam. With such strong competition for business, it was important to reduce journey times by any means possible.

The 'Eliza' reaches Glasgow

With fair weather and favourable winds the *Eliza* should reach Port Dundas at the Glasgow end of the canal within two weeks, stopping overnight at various ports on the East coast to load and unload cargo. The canal journey would take no longer than a day. At Port Dundas the square piano was to be collected by one of the Broadwood Glasgow agents and taken straight to the house in Miller Street, where Mrs Findlay would be eagerly awaiting its arrival.

The 'Eliza' disappears

The *Eliza* last appeared in *Lloyd's Register of Shipping* in 1807, when her rating had slipped to 'E1'. As the first element in the Lloyd's classification used vowels only, this meant that she had deteriorated only slightly, having slipped just one place from 'A' to 'E'.

5|—   Sp |A. Wilson| 71|Scotl'd|11|Capt. | 9|Lh Bones|E 1|99

The Eliza's last appearance in Lloyd's Register for 1807, her rating having slipped from 'A1' to 'E1'. Reproduced by permission of Lloyd's Register Information Centre.

She had thus become 'a vessel of the second class'; her disappearance from the Register may suggest that she was sold and renamed or, perhaps, lost at sea. Coincidentally, during most of the years the *Eliza* appeared in the Lloyd's Register, Findlay Bannatyne & Company were listed at the front of the Register among the 'Members of the Society'.

3. John Broadwood and the Square Piano

The Broadwood heritage

'John Broadwood & Sons Ltd' claims to be the oldest established piano company in the world. Its name is certainly one of the most prestigious. Broadwood instruments were enjoyed by such famous figures as Mozart, Haydn and Chopin. A particularly proud event in the company's history occurred in 1817 when Thomas Broadwood struck up a friendship with Beethoven in Vienna and offered him the gift of a piano. Beethoven gratefully accepted, writing to him in 1818 (in French):

'I shall look upon it as an altar upon which I shall place the most beautiful offerings of my spirit to the divine Apollo. As soon as I receive your excellent instrument, I shall immediately send you the fruits of the first moments of inspiration I spend at it, as a souvenir for you from me, my very dear B.; and I hope they will be worthy of your instrument'.

After Beethoven's death, the piano was given to Liszt who kept it in his library at Weimar. It had had a hammering during Beethoven's deafness and was in poor condition. In 1887 it found its way to the National Museum of Hungary in Budapest where, recently restored to its original condition by David Winston of the Period Piano Company in Kent, it remains today.

John Broadwood comes to London

The company's roots go back to 1761 when John Broadwood came to London aged 29, the eldest son of the village carpenter in Oldhamstocks in the Lothian Hills, south of Edinburgh. He came from solidly Protestant stock and remained a man of sincere religious principles and strong moral character throughout his life.

His early training as an apprentice in his father's carpentry shop, coupled with strong ambition and a natural aptitude for business, prepared him well for a successful career. It seems likely that after his apprenticeship he developed particular skills in the maintenance and repair of harpsichords in the Edinburgh area. To develop these further he would need to attach himself to a well-established musical instrument maker in London, where the most prestigious makers of the time were based.

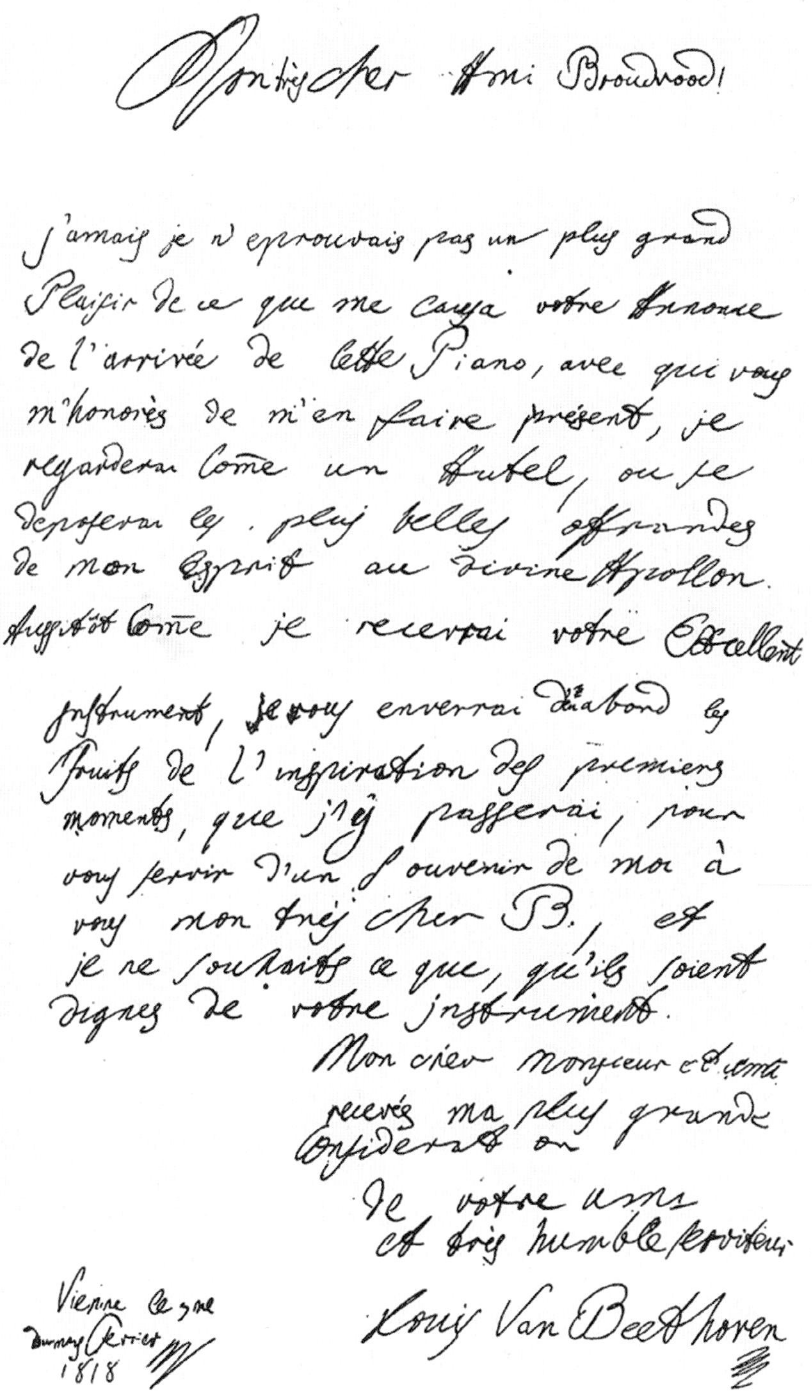

Montrès cher Ami Broadwood!

J'amais je n'eprouvais pas un plus grand
Plaisir de ce que me causa votre Annonce
de l'arrivée de cette Piano, avec qui vous
m'honorès de m'en faire présent, je
regarderai come un Autel, ou je
deposerai les plus belles offrandes
de mon Esprit au divine Apollon.
Aussitôt come je recevrai votre Excellent
instrument, je vous enverrai d'abord les
Fruits de l'inspiration des premiers
moments, que j'y passerai, pour
vous servir d'un Souvenir de moi à
vous mon trés cher B., et
je ne souhaite ce que, qu'ils soient
dignes de votre instrument.
            Mon cher Monsieur et amti
        recevés ma plus grande
    Consideration
        Je votre ami
        et trés humble serviteur.

        Louis Van Beethoven

Vienne le 3me
Durnay Février
1818

*Letter to Thomas
Broadwood
from Beethoven,
1818. From
The Musical Times,
15th December 1892.*

Burkat Shudi, his wife Catherine and sons Joshua (left) and Burkat, painted by Marcus Tuscher.
© National Portrait Gallery.

Broadwood joins Burkat Shudi

His technical ability, natural talent and personal qualities clearly impressed the Swiss harpsichord maker Burkat Shudi who in 1728 had set up his workshop near Golden Square in Soho. Shudi had become one of the great harpsichord makers of the 18th century, building instruments for the Prince of Wales and Frederick the Great. John Broadwood joined Shudi's business in Great Pulteney Street in September 1761 and became foreman responsible for the highly skilled task of making new soundboards for harpsichords.

Shudi's only surviving son, also called Burkat, worked for the family business too but it seems that he failed to demonstrate any of his father's technical ability or business acumen. Shudi Senior was now 59 and needed to plan for his succession. In the year that he took on John Broadwood, he also employed his nephew, another Joshua Shudi, perhaps with a 'Shudi' succession in mind. However, five years later Joshua left the firm and set up in business under his own Shudi name, leading to a serious rift with his uncle.

Broadwood joins the Shudi family

By 1769, with Joshua Shudi now established as an unwelcome competitor, John Broadwood had become a key figure in Burkat Shudi's business and had almost become a member of the family.

On 2nd January that year, Shudi, now aged 67, granted John Broadwood permission to marry his daughter Barbara who was then 19. A month later, on 9th February, the succession was effectively sealed when Shudi publicly announced that he had taken his new son-in-law into partnership. In March 1771, Shudi signed his entire business and the lease of his house in Great Pulteney Street over to Broadwood. He in turn agreed to pay Shudi an annuity of £25, together with various patent rights and an agreed share of profits on instrument repair and sales of new instruments.

A family in distress

Barbara Broadwood produced Burkat Shudi's first grandchild, named James Shudi Broadwood, in 1772. Now in failing health, the old man died the following year. Sadly she herself died in 1776 after a fourth pregnancy, leaving John Broadwood bereft, a widower with three young children and the whole business to run. Barbara's sister Margaret helped look after the children but then she too died in 1778, leaving him in an even more difficult situation.

Broadwood marries Mary Kitson

Three years later, however, just before Christmas 1781, John Broadwood, now 49, married for the second time. His new wife, Mary Kitson from Doncaster who was just 29, had been employed in the house, possibly as a governess. His marriage to a determined, energetic Yorkshirewoman 20 years his junior, transformed Broadwood's personal and business life. They soon started his 'second family'

of six children, born between 1782 and 1793. His renewed interest in the business focussed in particular on the technical development of square pianos and new approaches to selling them. The foundations of what was to become one of the world's most famous piano-making family businesses had now been firmly laid.

The development of the pianoforte

The invention of what we know as the piano, an instrument with hammers that hit the strings, is usually ascribed to the Italian Bartolomeo Cristofori (1655- 1731), musical instrument maker to the Medici. In England the earliest pianos looked very much like the harpsichords they were beginning to replace. With a harpsichord, where the string is plucked with a plectrum, the character and volume of the sound can be varied only by using different 'stops', by lifting the lid to various degrees, or by opening and closing horizontal shutters that operate on the Venetian blind principle. The new term 'pianoforte', or 'soft/loud', reflected the pianist's ability to play with a lighter or heavier touch. However, the early 'grand' pianos were expensive and not very responsive in the upper notes, so many musicians still preferred the clarity of the harpsichord.

John Zumpe invents the square piano

The future development of the piano was transformed by John Zumpe (the anglicized name of Johannes Zumpe, a German émigré from Saxony) who invented a much smaller rectangular keyboard instrument, to become known as the

John Zumpe square piano, 1772. Photo by kind permission of Saint Fagans National History Museum, Cardiff.

John Broadwood develops the square piano

John Broadwood saw a major new market in these square pianos and in 1778 produced some on an experimental basis. His first squares, very similar in shape and construction to the early Zumpe instruments, had carried the inscription *Burkat Shudi et Johannes Broadwood London fecerunt*, i.e. 'Burkat Shudi and John Broadwood made [it] in London', followed by the date and the Great Pulteney Street address. After his marriage to Mary Kitson, however, Shudi's name promptly disappeared: with her support, Broadwood was now his own man.

He decided that in a rapidly expanding market, the future of his business lay in adopting new methods of production and distribution. Instead of making instruments from scratch in his own works, he bought in components from specialist suppliers and used his team of highly skilled craftsmen to assemble and finish them to his exacting standards.

Always an innovator, he replaced hand-operated stops with pedals, making them easier to play and simpler to produce. Importantly, he protected his squares with his own patent.

Broadwood's network of agents

Broadwood also developed a new approach to sales and distribution. Rather than attracting potential customers to his London showroom, he set up contracts with a network of music shops and specialist retailers around Britain and Ireland.

square piano. Zumpe had worked for some time with Burkat Shudi in London but started his own business in December 1760, the year before John Broadwood joined Shudi's workshop. His growing reputation was such that the Mozart family visited his workshop in Prince's Street in 1764-65.

The oldest of Zumpe's surviving pianos dates from 1766. Simpler, smaller and cheaper than the early grand pianos, they were more domestic in scale. Measuring about five feet by three and supported on a light demountable frame, they had a special appeal among the emerging middle classes as they fitted easily into their parlours and were easy to move; also, when played with their lids down, they didn't annoy the neighbours. Their clear, sweet 'singing' tone, with the optional addition of various stops to produce different effects, made them very popular and demand for these instruments soon exceeded supply.

They would buy the instruments at a trade discount, cover the overheads of their own staff and showrooms and sell the pianos on at a profit. Broadwood insisted that all these instruments bore the *Broadwood* name, rather than those of the retailers, as was often the case with less prestigious piano makers.

Broadwood sent some of his early experimental models to William Ware of Belfast, with whom he had considerable trade. Ware held the post of organist at St Anne's Church, now St Anne's Church of Ireland Cathedral, for some 49 years.

Cutting the frets.

Key cutting.

Reproduced by permission of John Broadwood & Sons Ltd.

He was well known in the town's musical and educational circles and thus had a ready market for Broadwood instruments. Perhaps Broadwood thought it wise to test his prototype square pianos 'off-shore' first.

Jane Austen and the Broadwood square piano

The new trade in square pianos developed very quickly. Playing the piano and singing to entertain an audience were considered the hallmarks of a well-educated young gentlewoman.

This was reflected in the novels of Jane Austen, the great chronicler of that age: Broadwoods could not have had a better advertisement for their pianos. Her novels were filled with typical Broadwood customers, thus helping to stimulate even more sales among the fashion-conscious. Many of her heroines played the piano, as did she.

Typical Broadwood customers: Miss Harriet and Miss Elizabeth Binney, painted in 1806 by John Smart, 1742-1811. © Victoria and Albert Museum, London.

In *Emma*, for example, published in 1815, a Broadwood square piano played a key part in the plot when Frank Churchill ordered one to be sent anonymously to his secret fiancée Jane Fairfax, creating much gossip in Highbury:

'Mrs Cole was telling that she had been calling on Miss Bates, and as soon as she entered the room had been struck by the sight of a pianoforté – a very elegant looking instrument – not a grand, but a large-sized square pianoforté; and the substance of the story…was, that this pianoforté had arrived from Broadwoods the day before, to the great astonishment of aunt and niece…

'After dinner they have songs around the piano. At last Jane began, and although the first bars were feebly given, the powers of the instrument were gradually done full justice to. Mrs Weston had been delighted before, and was delighted again; Emma joined her in all her praise; and the pianoforté, with every proper discrimination, was pronounced to be altogether of the highest praise.'

John Broadwood retires: new partnerships emerge

In parallel with the development of square pianos, Broadwoods were also making grand pianos; by 1794 they had made over five hundred grands and a thousand squares, ample evidence that his new strategy was paying handsome dividends. The following year he took his son James Shudi Broadwood into partnership, aged 23; the company was now known as 'John Broadwood and Son'.

Engraving of a portrait of John Broadwood, aged 80, by John Harrison. Reproduced by permission of Surrey History Centre.

Having accumulated considerable wealth from these burgeoning sales, John Broadwood moved his wife and young family out of Great Pulteney Street, buying a much larger house in Kensington Gore. Aged 55, Broadwood was now well established as a highly successful businessman, enjoying the fruits of his labours, winning a respected position in society and gradually handing over more responsibility to his son.

In 1804, when Mrs Findlay bought her new square piano, James Shudi Broadwood was 32 and firmly in control of the day-to-day business of the company, while his father enjoyed his semi-retirement. When John Broadwood's third son,

Thomas, became a partner in 1808 at 23, the firm assumed the name of 'John Broadwood & Sons Ltd.'. It was this Thomas Broadwood who was to meet Beethoven in Vienna in 1817.

Thomas was in charge of the company's finances and paid particular attention to the detailed internal costings of the instruments. In December 1805, for example, the 'prime cost of a small pianoforte' was calculated at precisely £15.15s.3d. Mrs Findlay's instrument had cost £31.10s.0d, representing a 100% mark-up on the prime cost. The packing case and transport were extra. This was a profitable business.

Thomas Broadwood, 1786-1861, who arranged for a Broadwood Grand to be sent to Beethoven. Portrait by unknown artist, reproduced by kind permission of the Colt Clavier Collection.

The end of the square piano era

Broadwoods continued to make square pianos until 1866 but their heavier, ornate Victorian style never matched the simple elegance of Mrs Findlay's piano with its delicate French underframe. Thereafter, their growing international reputation would be based on building upright and grand pianos of the highest quality. After almost 150 years, the company changed hands in 2008, with Dr Alasdair Laurence as its new Chairman. It is now based at 'Finchcocks', a fine Georgian manor in Kent, which also houses a private collection of over 100 historic keyboard instruments. The company offers a comprehensive range of high quality hand-built instruments to order, and also a tuning and restoration service. It still holds the Royal Warrant as Pianoforte Manufacturers to the Queen. Almost 30 earlier, a younger Alasdair Laurence was to play an important part in the restoration of Mrs Findlay's Broadwood square piano.

'Broadwood by Appointment' - the Royal Warrant. Reproduced by permission of John Broadwood & Sons Ltd.

4. Mrs Findlay's Piano Appears in Ireland

An eligible young clergyman heads north

Gordon Hannon, the author's father, was born in 1891 in County Kildare. After graduating from Trinity College Dublin (TCD), he was ordained into the Anglican Church of Ireland. Following his first curacy in Dublin, he was asked to travel north to run the TCD Mission on the Shankill Road in Belfast. This was a tough job in a socially deprived area, during a difficult time in Irish politics, before partition.

He meets Hilda Denny

In late 1920, having successfully revived the TCD Mission, Gordon was appointed Rector of the market town of Ballymoney in County Antrim. Brought up in County Kildare, he enjoyed country pursuits and was a keen horseman. As an eligible clergyman, 30 years old, good-looking and single, he was frequently invited to social events around the county. At a *thé dansant* a young Hilda Denny, just 17 years old, caught his eye. They were married in April 1923; she was 19, he almost 32.

Gordon and Hilda Hannon's wedding day, 11th April 1923.

Hilda Denny's family

Hilda's father Leslie Denny was the youngest of Dumbarton shipbuilder Peter Denny's 13 children. As an engineer and Director of the family firm, Leslie Denny had worked on the development of marine engines, ship stability and paddle wheel design. Retiring early through ill health, Leslie Denny settled in County Antrim with his wife Frances and their young family, close to her family home.

Hilda's younger brother Edward, following family tradition, studied marine engineering and joined the firm, eventually becoming Chairman of Dennys in 1953.

LESLIE DENNY

Leslie Denny, retired Director of Dennys of Dumbarton, the author's grandfather.
Photo courtesy of Dumbarton Library Heritage Centre.

Making ends meet in retirement

In retirement, Hilda and Gordon went back to their County Antrim roots, finally settling in the seaside town of Ballycastle at the north-eastern corner of Ireland. Ballycastle Bay looks directly out to Rathlin Island, seven miles off-shore. The Mull of Kintyre is only fifteen miles away from the Irish coast and clearly visible in fine weather.

Gordon and Hilda Hannon's Golden Wedding Day, 11th April 1973, outside Billy Church, Co Antrim, where they were married in 1923.

Having raised five sons and a daughter, they had very little saved for their retirement. Gordon's church pension was so modest that new sources of supplementary income were needed. Always a very practical person, Hilda developed several innovative approaches to income generation. With the help of generous government loans, she devoted much of her time to restoring old farmhouses near Ballycastle, employing direct labour and acting as Clerk of Works. They lived in each house for a few years, sold up at a profit and moved to the next one - now known as 'property development'.

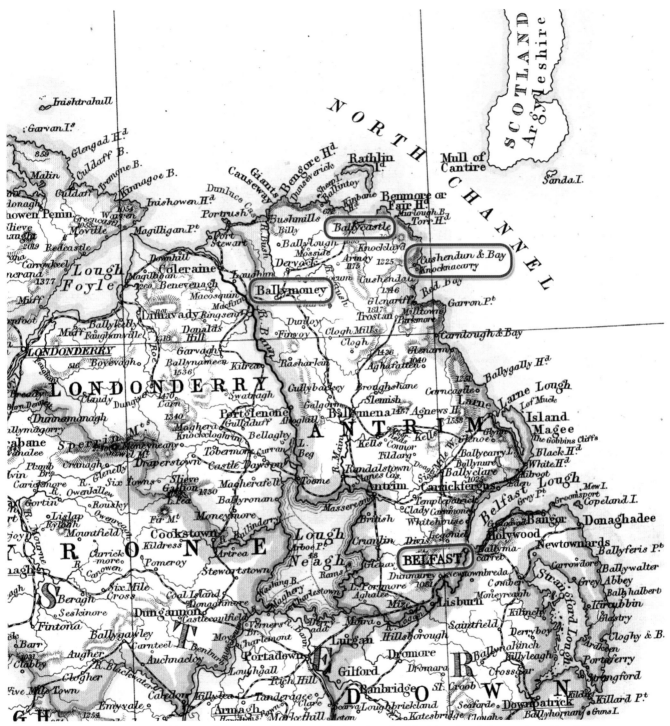

Map of Co. Antrim, showing Belfast, Ballycastle, Ballymoney, Cushendun, Rathlin Island and the southern tip of the Mull of Kintyre – here spelt 'Cantire'. From The XXth Century Citizens' Atlas of the World, ed. J. G. Bartholomew, ca. 1902. Image courtesy of Sheffield University Library.

P J McIlroy & Son's shop in Ballycastle in the 1970s.
Photographs reproduced by kind permission of Sean McIlroy.

P J McIlroy & Son's auction room.

P J McIlroy's Auction Room

Hilda also bought old furniture at auction, restoring and reselling it to supplement their income. One of her frequent haunts was PJ McIlroy's Auction Room in Ann Street, Ballycastle. Here she spent many hours buying and selling furniture and got to know Mr McIlroy, or 'PJ' as he was known locally. He always kept an eye out for furniture she might be interested in refurbishing.

'An old spinet'

In 1977, Hilda spotted what was described as 'an old spinet' in PJ's auction room. As a pianist she immediately recognized the famous name of Broadwood. Although the 'spinet' was in a distressed state, all the parts, including keys, strings and a wooden pedal seemed to be present. She thought that as I had some skills in cabinet making, I might enjoy restoring it - if she could buy it in the auction at a sensible price. In the previous week's sale the instrument had not reached its reserve of £50 so had been withdrawn pending further instruction from the vendor. PJ persuaded the vendor to sell it to Hilda for the £50, and she gave it to me.

A Broadwood square piano

The instrument turned out to be an 1804 Broadwood square piano, serial number 8119. It was delivered to my parents' house nearby. My father was then in his 86th year and in failing health. He quipped about not quite being ready yet for this 'coffin' which was kept in their bedroom; he died the following January.

Back across the Irish Sea

In July 1979 my wife and I took our then two young children on holiday to Ballycastle, towing a small trailer behind our Renault 6. For our return journey we carefully wrapped up the piano with blankets and plastic sheeting. We roped it securely into the trailer and brought it back by ferry across the Irish Sea via Stranraer to our house on the Wirral. Never had it made so fast a journey as we sped down the motorway.

Although unplayable and needing restoration, the little Broadwood had pride of place in our drawing room. We knew very little about Broadwood pianos, even less about 'square' ones.

5. Restoration

Initial assessment

After examining the piano closely I decided it was beyond my competence to restore it. I took advice from colleagues in the Music Department at Liverpool University and in August 1979 contacted Roy Knowles at Bolton Percy near Tadcaster in North Yorkshire. He had a reputation for authentic restoration and fine workmanship. My wife and I took the piano to him for his evaluation. While showing us round his workshop, he pointed to a square piano he was restoring for Lord Snowdon. The work was progressing beautifully, amply confirming his reputation for fine craftsmanship.

Roy Knowles' assessment of the piano

On 19th August 1979 Roy Knowles wrote: 'The piano is structurally very sound, no woodworm and no open glue lines, in fact nothing that would prevent a re-stringing to the original gauge and at one semi-tone below A440. The wrest-plank nut (the pinned bar where the strings pass from the wrest pins) has pulled away after many years but this can gradually be straightened and re-glued. A trial 'clean' on the case side suggests an ultimate colour very similar to the one you saw nearing completion. The hammers do not need re-covering and will clean thoroughly, but the pilot heads (on the ends of the keys that push up the hammers) will also need either re-covering with leather or remaking completely and this is as time-consuming as hammer covering. Two of the broken brass dampers I found under the key-frame, so only the 'rifles' need to be made. However, there will be much to do...'

Funding the restoration

For complete restoration he quoted £820 which seemed a very large sum for a piano bought at auction for £50. This was beyond our means at that stage. However, having seen Lord Snowdon's piano being beautifully restored in his workshop, we judged our project would be a good investment - but how could we fund it?

Several years earlier, when moving from one restored farmhouse to another, my parents had given various large pieces of furniture to members of the family. They gave one of my brothers a long Georgian D-end dining table; they gave us its twelve chairs, so we now had eighteen chairs and a small dining table. Six of the twelve were Sheraton and, even in poor condition, they each fetched £100 so we put the proceeds towards the restoration and asked Roy Knowles to proceed.

A. ROY KNOWLES
EARLY KEYBOARD INSTRUMENTS

REPRODUCTION SQUARE PIANOS - FORTEPIANOS   RESTORATIONS - TUNING - REPAIRS

19th August, 1979

Dear Mr. Hannon,

<u>Restoration of Broadwood Square, No.8119</u>

Having now made a close inspection of your piano, I can give you a better idea of what needs to be done to put the instrument into a fine playing condition and to put its' appearance into a state more in keeping with its' year, In fact, a restoration that should put it back to its' condition in say 1815, after a few years of careful use!

The piano is structurally very sound, no woodworm and no open glue lines, in fact nothing that would prevent a re-stringing to the original gauge and at one semi-tone below A 440.

The wrest-plank nut (the pinned bar where the strings pass from the wrest pins) has pulled away after many years, but this can be gradually straightened and re-glued. My rough estimate of £750-£900 can now be firmed at £820 and this figure will <u>not</u> be exceeded, and may be less.

If you can manage this I am sure you, and your wife, will be extremely pleased with the result and you can be certain to re-coup this money at the very least on re-sale. A trial 'clean' on the case side suggests an ultimate colour very similar to the one you saw nearing completion. The hammers, also, do not need re-covering and will clean thoroughly. <u>But</u>, the pilot heads (on the ends of the keys that push up the hammers) will all need either re-covering with leather or re-making completely and this is as time-consuming as hammer covering. Two of the broken brass dampers I found under the key-frame, so only the 'rifles' need to be made. However, there will be much to do and attched I have detailed the work necessary.

Perhaps you would be kind enough to let me know fairly soon whether we can proceed.

Yours faithfully,

A.Roy Knowles

Roy Knowles' letter of 19th August 1979, including quotation for the restoration; reproduced by his kind permission.

Restoration and restringing

He stripped the piano completely, cleaning and refurbishing all the hammers and leathers. He used new strings specially ordered from the piano-maker Alasdair Laurence who, some thirty years later, was to become Chairman of Broadwoods. These included bass strings open-wrapped with silver-plated covering wire, and new brass and steel wire for the rest, as in the original. He repolished the case and the 'French' underframe. Four new brass medallions to cover the ends of the long bolts holding the underframe together were specially cast from the surviving originals using the lost-wax process. He replaced the missing return-spring wire that connects the wooden pedal to the damper rail.

After stripping and repolishing the name board, he relined the back of its delicate fretwork designs with new turquoise silk. The refurbished keyboard ivories and ebonies set off the completed job beautifully.

Valuation

In April 1980 we paid Roy Knowles' bill and brought the superbly restored Broadwood back to West Kirby, together with some spare strings left over from the new set made by Alasdair Laurence. He valued it for insurance purposes at £1,950. It had been a good investment.

Mrs Findlay's square piano after restoration.
Photo: © 2014 Kirsty Prince.

A. ROY KNOWLES
EARLY KEYBOARD INSTRUMENTS

REPRODUCTION SQUARE PIANOS - FORTEPIANOS   RESTORATIONS - TUNING - REPAIRS

August 20
1979

Valuation of Broadwood Square Piano
dated 1804 , No 8119 for Mrs. Mannon

For insurance purposes only   £ 1950

AR Knowles

Roy Knowles' valuation of the restored piano; reproduced by his kind permission.

6. Initial Broadwood Research

A letter to Broadwoods

In March 1980 I wrote to Broadwoods, then based in Acton and still mass producing pianos, to find out if there was any record of the original owner of the piano. The original 8119 serial number,

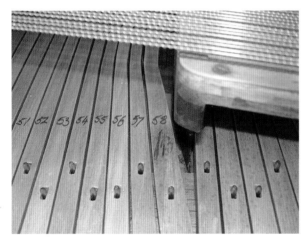

Initials 'JB' on key lever 58.

clearly written in Indian ink at the back of the piano to the right behind the tuning pins, and the 1804 date on the name board would surely provide a link to the original sale record if it still existed.

The initials 'JB' were also written in Indian ink on the hidden part of key lever 58, the D natural two octaves above Middle C: might they be the initials of the key-cutter, the workshop foreman - or perhaps even James Shudi Broadwood?

In my letter I commented on the rather roughly carved hole between key levers 19 and 20 (for the B and C naturals an octave below Middle C) to allow the pedal wire to reach the damper rail.

Serial number 8119 - a vital clue.
Photo: © 2014 Kirsty Prince.

The hole between key levers 19 and 20, with pedal wire attached to hook on damper rail.

was *not* the case, as the original sale documentation shows that the pedal was fitted as an original optional extra - see Chapter 1]. At a recent Sotheby sale one of these instruments made in 1807 fetched a price of £1,000 so for insurance purposes we suggest that you have it covered for this price plus 50% to allow for replacement value'. It was disappointing that there seemed little chance of finding out any further information about the original owner.

'Broadwood by Appointment: a History'

It wasn't until some 20 years later that I discovered David Wainwright's *Broadwood by Appointment: a History,* officially commissioned by Broadwoods

JOHN BROADWOOD & SONS LTD

APPOINTED PIANOFORTE MANUFACTURERS
TO
KING GEORGE II

KING GEORGE III	KING GEORGE IV
KING WILLIAM IV	QUEEN VICTORIA
KING EDWARD VII	QUEEN ALEXANDRA
KING GEORGE V	QUEEN MARY
KING GEORGE VI	

BY APPOINTMENT
TO HER MAJESTY THE QUEEN
PIANOFORTE MANUFACTURERS

BY APPOINTMENT
TO HER MAJESTY QUEEN ELIZABETH
THE QUEEN MOTHER
PIANOFORTE TUNERS

Pianoforte Makers
ESTABLISHED 1728

WORKS, TUNING & REPAIRS DEPT.
1-5 BRUNEL ROAD
LONDON W3 7UG
TELEPHONE : 01-743 5804
01-743 6657   01-749 1337

SALES & SHOWROOM
56-57 CONDUIT ST.
LONDON W1R 9FD
TELEPHONE : 01-439 1714
REGISTERED : NO 71504 ENGLAND
Ref:SEHB

M. S-M. Hannon,
11, Belmont Road,
West Kirby,
Wirral,
Merseyside L48 5EY.   2nd April 1980

Dear Sir,

In reply to your letter dated the 25th March concerning the piano in your possession, we regret that we are unable to give you details of th original owner of this instrument as the records do not exist.

We can, however, confirm the date as being 1804. The pedal is not original but instruments of this period often had forte pedals added at a later date which explains the rather crude workmanship.

At a recent Sotheby Sale one of these instruments made in 1807 fetched a price of £1000 so for insurance purposes we suggest that you have it covered for this price plus 50% to allow for replacement value.

Yours faithfully,

S. E. H. Broadwood
Sales Director.

Letter from Stuart Broadwood. 2nd April 1980: 'the records do not exist'.

The reply from Broadwoods

In April, Mr S[tuart] E W Broadwood, Sales Director, wrote back:

'We regret that we are unable to give you details of the original owner of this instrument as the records do not exist. We can, however, confirm the date as being 1804. The pedal is not original but instruments of this period often had forte pedals added at a later date which explains the rather crude workmanship. [Author's note: this

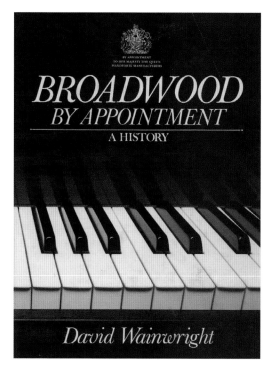

'Broadwood by Appointment: a History',
by David Wainwright.
Reproduced by permission of
John Broadwood & Sons Ltd.

and published in 1982. Intriguingly, Wainwright referred to the Broadwood 'porters' books' which recorded the movement of instruments in and out of the factory. When Stuart Broadwood wrote to me in 1980, he must have been aware of these books as they were a major source for Wainwright's then forthcoming official history. As his letter had said that 'the records do not exist', I assumed the specific porters' book for my piano was missing. The trail had gone cold.

'Broadwood Square Pianos', by Michael Cole, reproduced by permission of the author.

'Broadwood Square Pianos'

In May 2007 I came across Michael Cole's crucially important new book *Broadwood Square Pianos*, published in 2005. He traces the development of square pianos in meticulous detail from their early

development by John Zumpe to their later refinement by John Broadwood. He also frequently refers to the porters' books and other records in the Broadwood Archive in the Surrey History Centre in Woking. Perhaps after all there might still be some record of my piano hidden away undiscovered.

The Broadwood Archives

In 1977 the Broadwood Archives had been rescued from the disused former home of the late Captain Evelyn Broadwood, Chairman of the firm in the 1930s. Many of the records stored in outbuildings suffered serious damage from dampness and mould. Now held in the Surrey History Centre in Woking, the surviving archive comprises ledgers from 1794, daybooks (the porters' books) from 1798, and production, promotional and sales records; it is the most comprehensive set of records for any musical instrument-making firm.

A Heritage Lottery Grant enabled the Centre to conserve 35 archive volumes, including 31 day books and their associated number books. Each piano the firm made bears a unique serial number and these records identify the piano and details of its sale or hiring. Also conserved are a letter book of 1801-1810 providing evidence of the firm's international activities and a book into which brochures and a price list were inserted, which shows the range of pianos and the development and costing of models. A detailed catalogue of the entire archive has been completed and the original volumes are available for consultation by members of the public in the Centre's reading room.

The company changes hands

In late 2009 I discovered that 'John Broadwood & Sons Ltd, Pianoforte Makers' had changed hands in 2008. The last Chairman from the Broadwood family had been the Stuart Broadwood who had written to me nearly thirty years earlier in 1980. The company still retained the Royal Warrant as Pianoforte Manufacturers to the Queen. Their new website offered a fee-based search service of the Broadwood Archives for details of instruments for which there were serial numbers and dates. I filled in their online form and sent off my cheque for £50, more in hope than expectation.

We meet Mrs Findlay

A whole new research trail opened up when Alasdair Laurence, the new Chairman of the company, wrote to me on 12th December 2009:

'We now have pleasure in providing all the information we can find in our company records about your Broadwood square piano with the serial number 8119. The earliest reference we can find to your piano is contained in one of our porters' books, and is dated 10th July 1804. On that day, your piano was transported from our workshops to a certain Mrs Findlay, who was staying with a Mrs Bannatine at 8, New Broad Street in the City of London. The piano was sent 'on approval' for her to try, with a view to possible purchase or hire. The two porters who moved your piano are named in our records as Mr Clark and Mr Chandler.

'Evidently, Mrs Findlay decided to purchase the instrument. It was brought back to our warehouse, checked over, regulated and tuned, and placed in a special wooden packing case. On 10th August 1804, your piano was taken by our porters to Glasgow Wharf, Port of London, in order for it to be transported to Scotland on the sailing ship *Eliza*. We even have the name of the ship's master in our records: he was Captain Alexander Wilson.

'The final delivery point of your piano was the home of Mrs Findlay, Miller Street, Glasgow. We assume that Mrs Findlay, a resident of Glasgow, had been visiting London, and took the opportunity to choose a new piano during her visit to the capital.

'After the 10th August, your square piano disappears from our records, and so we regret that the amount of information we can provide is rather limited. Nevertheless, we hope that you find the details enclosed with this letter to be of use and interest.

'In answer to your question about a valuation, it is almost impossible for us to value an instrument we have not seen. We can tell you, however, that at the present time squares are not fetching particularly good prices compared with some years ago. At a London auction room you could expect to buy an unrestored square of the same age as yours for around £1,000 or even less, and a fully restored one for between £2,000 and £3,000.'

I was back on the trail.

7. Who was Mrs Findlay?

The house on Miller Street

Mrs Findlay lived in Miller Street in Glasgow, but there was no house number given in the Broadwood porters' book. The Mitchell Library in Glasgow held a postal directory for 1804 but it consisted of one simple A-Z list of people's names showing where they lived in the city, rather than lists of streets with numbered houses and their occupants. The only 'Findlay' entry was for a Doctor Robert Findlay, Professor of Divinity at Glasgow University, with his address given as 'the College'. There was no hint of any Findlays living in Miller Street.

Robert Findlay, the 8th of Boturich

An internet search using the terms 'Findlay', 'Miller Street', and 'Glasgow' immediately turned up the transcript of an interview which Robert

'Dr Robert Findlay, Professor of Divinity' entry in 1804 Glasgow postal directory.
© CSG CIC Glasgow Museums and Libraries Collection: The Mitchell Library, Special Collections.

Findlay, 'the 8th of Boturich', had given to a Sarah Powell under the aegis of *Burke's Peerage and Gentry* in 2001. The interview covered this Robert Findlay's life story: he had commanded a company of Ghurkhas and been wounded in Burma during the war with the Japanese. Now retired from his own business in Glasgow, he was living at Knockour, near Balloch, beside Loch Lomond. The transcript also gave an outline of his family history as far back as 1547.

'Easterhill', bought by Robert Findlay in 1783. Photograph taken in 1870 by Thomas Annan, courtesy of Glasgow University Library Special Collections.

42 Miller Street and 'Easterhill'

Crucially for my research, the interview transcript had a specific Findlay reference to number 42 in Glasgow's Miller Street. This was a grand town house which his ancestor, another Robert Findlay, had bought in 1784 at the age of only 36, having made his fortune in the Virginia tobacco plantations.

In 1783 this Robert Findlay had also bought *Easterhill*, a magnificent country house three miles up the Clyde on the London Road, east of Glasgow.

No. 42 Miller Street, Glasgow: 'The Tobacco Merchant's House', bought by Robert Findlay in 1784. © Joe Sheldon.

Could this Robert Findlay, known as 'The Tobacco Merchant', have been related to Professor Findlay at the University or to our Mrs Findlay? If he was her husband, why was *his* name not also listed in the 1804 street directory as living in Miller Street?

TD Findlay in partnership with Peter Denny

The transcript later describes how one of the tobacco merchant's grandsons, Thomas Dunlop ('TD') Findlay, an entrepreneurial timber and rice merchant, had set up a company 'TD Findlay and Son Ltd, East India Merchants' in 1839, with yards in Moulmein, across the Bay of Martaban from Rangoon in Lower Burma. To my astonishment, I read that he had gone into partnership with the Dumbarton shipbuilder Peter Denny - my great-grandfather.

The Irrawaddy Flotilla

TD Findlay and Peter Denny's greatest achievement was the creation of the 'Irrawaddy Flotilla', a fleet of flat-bottomed boats which plied their trade the length of the Irrawaddy. These steam-powered vessels were prefabricated in Peter Denny's Dumbarton shipyard and other Clyde yards, then shipped out to Burma where they were reassembled. By the Second World War the Flotilla had grown to some 650 vessels. This Findlay/Denny family connection, revealed through my mother's chance purchase of a Broadwood square piano at a country auction in Ireland, was an extraordinary coincidence.

First contact with Mrs Findlay's great, great, great-grandsons

When I contacted Robert Findlay, the 8th of Boturich, his wife Liisa confirmed that I had found the right person but she explained that her husband had had a stroke the previous year. His brother Bill, who lived nearby, had taken over his role as family historian and could help with my research.

On 11th March 2010 I received the following letter from Bill Findlay:

'Liisa Findlay, my sister-in-law, has passed your letter on to me as Robert, my elder brother, is getting a bit vague. Thanks to his excellent genealogical work in the past I can answer all your questions.

'Firstly may I say that my wife Delia and I owe a lot to your Uncle Edward [Denny]. In 1962 he sold 'Auchenlinnhe' to us, where we have lived very happily ever since; it has been a wonderful home to us and our three children. So you see that it was a great pleasure to get your letter, which also is of special interest as the piano has a very romantic story attached to it.

'My three greats-grandfather, Robert Findlay, a Virginia Tobacco Merchant, returned to Glasgow from America and bought 42 Miller Street in 1784. His wife Dorothy, née Dunlop, purchased the piano while staying with her daughter Janet, who had married John Bannatyne, merchant of London. Robert and Dorothy also had a younger daughter called Dorothy [later known as 'Dorothea']. She fell in love with her music teacher, no doubt over the keys of the piano, running away to marry him in 1820. This caused much anger from her parents, the lawsuits still being fought till old Robert's [her brother's] death in 1862.

'As the music teacher, John Donaldson, went on to be Professor of Music at Edinburgh University, I cannot see what the parents had to complain about. I think it was a case of Findlay arrogance, not an unknown commodity. That the romantic piano should appear to us 190 years after the romance is fascinating to me - it warrants at least a novel. We would be delighted if you could come and stay with us at Auchenlinnhe when you come to Glasgow in April. It would be wonderful to have Edward Denny's nephew stay in what I still refer to as Edward's house. Please come.'

Bill Findlay had now confirmed that Mrs Findlay's home was indeed 42 Miller Street, that she had been the widow of Robert Findlay, the Virginia tobacco merchant, and that her grandson TD Findlay had gone into business with my great-grandfather Peter Denny. A link with the Professor Findlay at Glasgow University was still to emerge [*see* the Findlay and Denny family trees inside front cover].

Staying at 'Auchenlinnhe'

It was another remarkable coincidence that Bill and Delia Findlay had bought my Uncle Edward Denny's house. My wife and I took up their invitation and stayed at Auchenlinnhe, enjoying

'Auchenlinnhe', the house which Edward Denny, the author's uncle, sold to Bill and Delia Findlay. Photograph reproduced with their kind permission.

Bill and Delia Findlay in their summerhouse at Auchenlinnhe. Photograph reproduced with their kind permission.

their generous hospitality. We were also kindly entertained by Robert and Liisa Findlay. Sadly Robert Findlay died just a year later.

Boturich Castle

Bill and Delia Findlay took us to Boturich Castle which had been the Findlay family home for many years. The 'Boturich' title had come down through the Findlay family from TD Findlay's eldest brother, another Robert Findlay (1812-1850). The title,

Boturich Castle today.
Photograph reproduced by kind permission of Laura Peat.

The late Robert Findlay, 8th of Boturich, with his wife Liisa, outside their home near Boturich Castle in 2010. Photograph reproduced by kind permission of Liisa Findlay.

which was not directly hereditary, had now reached Robert, 'the 8th of Boturich'. He and Liisa Findlay had built a new house in the grounds of Boturich Castle which, no longer in Findlay hands, is now both a family home and a superb wedding venue on the banks of Loch Lomond.

The Findlay 'Red Book' and the Dumbarton Archives

Bill Findlay introduced us to the Findlay family history known as 'The Red Book' (*An Leabhar Dearg* in Gallic). This key document had been typed up from a 19th century family manuscript and was now available on the web. We also went to the Dumbarton Archives where we made copies of the Findlay family tree going back to the late 16th century and had access to the extensive Denny Archives also held there. Together with the

digital resources of the *Scotland's People* digital archive on the web, there was now ample information to take the story forward.

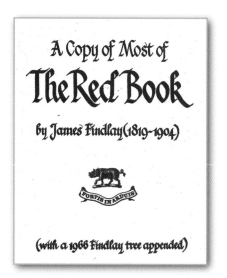

The Findlay Red Book, reproduced by kind permission of Bill Findlay.

8. Mrs Findlay's family

Mrs Findlay's husband Robert Findlay, Tobacco Merchant

Born in 1748, Robert Findlay had set sail for Virginia in 1764, aged just 16, to join two uncles already well established in the tobacco trade. He had swiftly made his fortune in four years and returned to establish himself in business in Glasgow in 1768. He married Dorothy Dunlop in Paisley Abbey on 21st July 1781; in the Parish Register recording their marriage, her name is given as 'Dorothy', rather than her baptismal name 'Dorretty'.

They bought Easterhill in 1783 and 42 Miller Street a year later. The house in Miller Street doubled as the family's town house and Robert's business premises. It was his father, Rev Dr Robert Findlay, Professor of Divinity at Glasgow University, who was listed in the 1804 postal directory as 'at the College'; it was he who had sent his young son out to join his uncles in Virginia. These uncles, Alexander and William *Cunningham*e, were actually *half*-brothers to Dr Findlay.

According to the Red Book, Robert the Tobacco Merchant died in a riding accident on 5th May 1802, either hitting his head on an overhanging tree or his horse having rolled on him after a fall. This explained why *his* name hadn't appeared in the 1804 Glasgow postal directory.

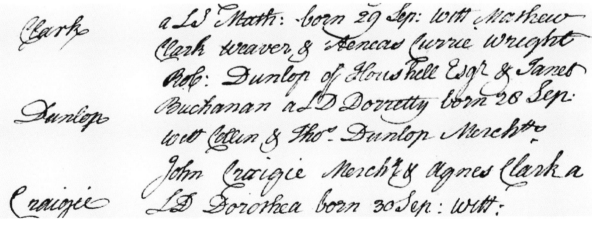

Dorothy Dunlop's 2nd October 1759 baptismal record, showing her baptismal name as 'Dorretty'.
© Crown copyright.

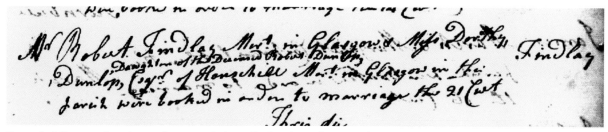

*Record of the marriage banns between Robert Findlay, 'Merchant in Glasgow',
and Dorothy Dunlop at Renfrew, 9th July 1781.
© Crown copyright.*

The Findlay Children

Robert and Dorothy Findlay had five children: Janet (b. 1782), Robert (b. 1784, at 42 Miller Street), Annabella (b. 1787), an infant Dorothy (who died at six days old in 1789) and another Dorothy (b. 1792), known later as 'Dorothea'.

Janet Findlay

Janet, the eldest of the family, married John Bannatyne, a London merchant of Scottish family, on 21st March 1803 when she was 20. Her grandfather, Rev Dr Findlay, officiated at their wedding in Glasgow. Her husband, John Bannatyne, had been in partnership with her late father, trading as 'Findlay Bannatyne & Co' in Throgmorton Street, London.

The newly married Bannatynes lived at 8, New Broad Street, London. Thus the Mrs 'Bannatine' that Mrs Findlay was staying with in July/August 1804 was her eldest daughter Janet. Mrs Findlay had travelled from Glasgow to London to stay with Janet when she was expecting her first baby. The baptismal records show that the baby was christened 'Dorothea' in the Scotch Church, London Wall on 10th August 1804; this,

coincidentally, was the very date that Mr Evans, the Broadwood porter, collected Mrs Findlay's piano for packing and sending on to Captain Wilson's sailing ship *Eliza* in the Port of London.

An entry in the porters' book for the *previous* year recorded the delivery of Broadwood square piano serial number 7339 to a Mr Bannatyne at No. 8, New Broad Street, on 23rd May 1803. As the ledger entry was in *his* name, it seems possible that he had bought it as a surprise wedding present for Janet on return from their honeymoon.

It also seems that Janet was so pleased with *her* Broadwood that she persuaded her mother to have another on approval during her stay in London. As the upbringing of Janet's younger sisters Annabella and Dorothea in Glasgow also required a good musical education, Mrs Findlay would have needed little persuasion.

John and Janet Bannatyne's second child, Charles, arrived a year after his sister Dorothea in 1805. He went to Balliol, entered the Church and became Rector of Aldham, Essex from 1840-82. His elder sister Dorothea never married and eventually

Brass plaque under the stained glass windows in Aldham Parish Church commemorating John and Janet Bannatyne.

went to live in Aldham with Charles and his wife (their first cousin and yet another Dorothea). They must both have inherited considerable wealth from their parents as they contributed much to the rebuilding of Aldham Parish Church and the building of the almshouses which still stand in the village.

Their parents John and Janet Bannatyne are commemorated in two stained-glass windows in the Church.

Robert [later known as 'the Banker']

Robert, second in Mrs Findlay's family, had graduated from Glasgow with an MA in 1802, the year his father died. After some years trying to hold the family business together, he went on to a new and successful career in banking: he was to be known in the family history as 'Robert the Banker'. He was also to play a central part in his youngest sister Dorothea's future legal and financial affairs.

Annabella

Robert's younger sister Annabella married John Thomas Alston, a Glasgow merchant in 1810 and they went on to have seven children. He was Lord Provost in 1822 when George IV visited Scotland and thus represented Glasgow at the Court of Holyrood. In 1826 Annabella and her husband left Glasgow and settled in Liverpool.

'The Flighty Dorothea'

Robert's youngest 'pet' sister Dorothea, known by later Findlay generations, perhaps unkindly, as 'The Flighty Dorothea', was to become a central character in the Findlay family saga over the next half-century. Dorothea's father had died intestate in 1802, when she was only ten years old. Under Scottish law, she was still 'in her pupilarity', requiring her to have a 'tutor' or special guardian, to look after her legal and financial interests. The person appointed was John Bannatyne, who had been her father's managing partner in Findlay Bannatyne & Company and was to marry her elder sister Janet the following year. Her grandfather, Rev Dr Findlay, acted as 'cautioner' or surety for John Bannatyne as Dorothea's tutor until his death in 1814 when her brother Robert [the Banker] took over this responsibility – one which was to prove so heavy in the years ahead.

Piano lessons at 42 Miller Street

When the piano was delivered to 42 Miller Street in Glasgow in August 1804, Robert was 20, Annabella 17 and Dorothea just 12 years old. The family would have spent most of their time living out at Easterhill, where they would already have had a larger piano or harpsichord. Once a week, Mrs Findlay would have taken her younger daughters the three miles into town to have their piano lessons on the new Broadwood in their Miller Street townhouse.

Annabella and Dorothea were at an age when Mrs Findlay needed to keep a watchful eye on them and, not least, their piano teacher. Lessons over, they would have gone shopping in town, buying new music and visiting their dressmaker to choose the latest fashionable designs. After lunch with Robert, who was now heavily involved in the family business and lived in their Miller Street townhouse during the week, their carriage would have taken them back to Easterhill.

Little did Mrs Findlay realize how significant her purchase of the Broadwood square piano - and especially Dorothea's piano lessons - would turn out to be for the whole family over the next half century.

The Piano Lesson, late 18th century. By kind by permission of David Winston and The Period Piano Company.

9. Rev Professor Robert Findlay DD, 'The Doctor'

Minister and theologian

Robert Findlay, Mrs Findlay's father-in-law, was born in 1721. He was referred to by his descendents as 'The Doctor' and in his later years filled the role of *pater familias*. He graduated from Glasgow University with an MA in 1737 and continued his theological studies in Leiden, London and possibly the University of Edinburgh. He became a Church of Scotland minister in 1744. Following several earlier posts, in 1756 he became Minister of St David's Church, the 'Ramshorn Kirk' in Glasgow's 'Merchant City', where the wealthy tobacco merchants had their warehouses and residences.

Professor and Dean of Faculty

As a theologian he had a strong record of academic publishing and received the degree of Doctor Divinity (DD) from the University of Glasgow in 1776. Two years later he applied for the University Chair of Divinity but was unsuccessful. He was finally appointed to it when the previously successful candidate died in 1782. He also served as Dean of Faculty. He held his Chair until his death on 15th June 1814, aged 93.

The affection of his students

Professor Findlay was known for delivering 'a rambling course of prelections [lectures] of portentous range and elaborate execution' but he was also a man who had the best interests of his students at heart. In 1800 he stood fast against the introduction of class fees for divinity students. In an obituary, a Dr Strang wrote: 'A figure, never very large, but shrunk and attenuated by age, was surmounted by a full-bottomed wig and cocked hat, under the weight of which he seemed to totter. But his mild eye and benevolent expression of countenance secured the deference of the citizens and the affections of his students; while his learning and liberality, and his courteous and kind demeanour, inspired the latter at once with reverence and gratitude'.

Academic and prolific publisher

The central theme of Professor Findlay's academic publications was to uphold the divine inspiration of the scriptures. In 1763, he wrote *A Persuasive to the enlargement of Psalmody: or, attempt to show the reasonableness, and obligation of joining with the Psalms of David, other scriptural songs, especially out of the New Testament, By a*

Rev Professor Dr Robert Findlay. Oil on canvas by Peter Paillou (the Younger), 1807.
© The Hunterian, University of Glasgow, 2013.

Minister of the Church of Scotland. This classic title was republished as a paperback facsimile in 2010.

In 1770 he wrote a colossal and perhaps his best known work of some 600 pages: *A vindication of the sacred books...from various misrepresentations and cavils of the celebrated M. Voltaire.* This was also published as a classic paperback facsimile in 2012.

His last work, *The Divine Inspiration of the Jewish Scriptures or Old Testament,* published in 1803, was re-published as a full-text electronic facsimile in 2013. It is clear that he is still regarded today as a major figure in 18th century theological scholarship.

His son Robert sails to Virginia

On 24th April 1745 Robert Findlay, the rising cleric and theologian, married his cousin Annabella Paterson. They had three children of whom Robert, the eldest, was the only one to survive childhood; he was born on 17th January 1748 and baptised in Galston, Ayrshire, presumably by his father where he was Minister at the time. On 11th August 1764, after schooling in Glasgow, the young Robert, just 16 years old, sailed from Liverpool to Falmouth, Virginia, to join his two uncles. His anxious father and mother had travelled down to Liverpool to see him safely off. His father gave him the following touching letter to deliver to his uncle Alexander Cunninghame:

Virginia preferable to the Portuguese Papists

'Dear Brother, This comes by my son and your nephew whom I never intended as a messenger over the Atlantick, but I desire to submit to the management of an all wise providence an attachment to you which I believe has grown up since you used at Kilmarnock to indulge him in his childish sports and amusements, and a sight of that spendor and magnificence in which some persons live with so often the pursuit of trade for a while in one or other American region have, I fancy, conspired to produce in him so strong and violent an inclination that I did not think it safe to thwart it but judged it advisable to yield to it amidst all the resistance of nature. Nor did I repent my consent to his visiting your American region in preference to Lisbon to which you rather point in your letter by Captain Ewing. That city hath at different times [been]...a scene of much misery and distress, and sad as you may be, I do not think he would be safe in his principles and morals among Portugese Papists.

Wisdom and virtue before wealth

'The low state of the tobacco trade hath been reckoned by some a discouragement. But all trades have seasons of stagnation and it is hoped it will revive. Besides I am not so solicitous of his becoming rich and wealthy as for his being a wise and virtuous man, for which I can at least rely he will be better situated under your care and control than I could was he placed with a stranger. I cannot

THE

DIVINE INSPIRATION

OF THE

JEWISH SCRIPTURES,

OR

OLD TESTAMENT,

ASSERTED BY

St. PAUL, 2 TIMOTHY, iii. 16.

AND

DR. GEDDES'S REASONS AGAINST THIS SENSE

OF HIS WORDS EXAMINED.

———◆———

By ROBERT FINDLAY, D.D.

PROFESSOR OF THEOLOGY IN THE UNIVERSITY OF GLASGOW.

———◆———

LONDON:

PRINTED BY A. STRAHAN, PRINTERS-STREET,

FOR T. CADELL JUN. AND W. DAVIES IN THE STRAND.

1803.

Title page from Prof Findlay's 'Divine Inspiration of the Jewish Scriptures or Old Testament', published in 1803.

doubt you will be careful to instruct him as a merchant. It is my desire he may prove a sober and diligent and submissive assistant while at the same time he is careful to improve his intervals of leisure as attention to your business allows.

Robert's moral welfare

'I beg therefore you may detain him at least for a good time with yourself instead of sending him into any store under another master...What sort of lads your assistants are, I know not; possibly they are mixed. You will oblige me by placing him in bed and chamber with one of the most innocent and wise and amiable among them, but still more if you admit him into any apartment with yourself, or where he will be solitary but at your hand.

Keeping the Lord's Day

'The Lord's Day I understand is the day when you all traffic with the negroes for eggs and other necessities of life, but I am afraid [I] am not content with this barter which may soon [lead to an] over-neglect to Sunday...This you may well suppose I cannot approve. It is my earnest charge to him that he may be regular at his attendance on public worship, whatever diversity there may be in the form from that to which he hath been accustomed, and that he in other respects redeem time on that day for impressing a sense of religious truths and moral obligations on his heart....

A soft and smooth word in private

'I have not been negligent to give him such advices as occurred to me he might approve himself worthy in that station, which if providence conduct him to you he is to fill...I entreat you may also bestow particular attention upon his being a good and prudent man. A soft and smooth word in private I have often observed is by his natural temper more effectual with him than rougher address. He is free from all vice so far as I know, and I think I have been pretty watchful over him. But he is young and may soon be seduced by the [ways] of wicked men. I pray God he may not be and beg you may supply my place to him, by [wise] counsels and advice. In case he does not enjoy good health he has it in charge to return.

'In loco parentis'

'Also if the country is disagreeable to him it will give us no pain that he come back, as parting from him is no small affection. I pray God to watch over him and you in whose health and safety I am now more than ever interested for his sake. You will find most of the father in this letter, whose bowels you are not supposed yet to experience, but if you put yourself in imagination in my circumstances, you'll excuse it at present. I am sure that whenever you are a father in like situation you'll have in your own breast an abundant apology for the tenderest parts of it.

A sorrowful separation

'His mother desired me to present her compliments to you and to tell you that she expects you'll be particularly attentive to his virtue. You must not neglect with your own hand to inform me how he does and to admonish him to remember us by some lines longer or shorter on every occasion. I particularly [ask that] he will notify his arrival in the quickest method you can direct. Wishing you all happiness, I am, dear brother, in the near prospect of a sorrowful separation from the bearer…

Your most affectionate brother, Robert Findlay. Liverpool. August 11, 1764.'

'Bob' Findlay returns to Glasgow

It was a very difficult time for Robert and Annabella as they might never see their only surviving child again. They must have been greatly relieved four years later when the following letter arrived from Alexander Cunninghame in July 1768:

'Dear Brother, I have the pleasure to inform you that your son and me arrived this day about one o'clock at Port Glasgow in the 'Cunninghame', both in good health. Bob's horse, not being so good as mine, I pushed forward to town hoping to overtake [reach] W.C. [Bob's uncle William] before he went out, and have embraced the opportunity which my being ahead of him puts in my power to advise you of Bob's arrival, that you may take your own prudent way of acquainting Mrs Findlay, lest his sudden appearance may have some violent effect on her spirits. He will be here about fifteen minutes or thirty minutes hence. You may therefore expect him in that time. Should you choose to walk out or send a line for him here. I push immediately out to my brother's, and shall do myself the pleasure of seeing you tomorrow. I would call now but am aware that my presence would have the same effect on Mrs Findlay as Bob's and probably worse, he not being come up.

I am, Dr Sir, Your's Affectely, Alex Cunninghame. Argyle Street, Cochranes Compy's Counting House'.

Thus it was only four years later that the young 'Bob' Findlay returned to Glasgow with his Uncle Alexander and was safely home again with his much relieved parents. He was now a wealthy young man ready to build on his success in the world of tobacco trading and establish himself in Glasgow society.

Dr Findlay loses his only son

It was one of the tragedies of Dr Findlay's long life that, having lost two children in their infancy, he was to outlive his surviving son who died in 1802, by another twelve years. However, during those years he continued to play a key part in the life of the extended Findlay family, as devoted father-in-law to his son's widow Dorothy, and much loved grandfather to her children. He died in 1814 aged 93.

10. Robert Findlay, 'The Tobacco Merchant'

The Glasgow tobacco trade

By the time the young Robert Findlay set off for Virginia in 1764, the Glasgow tobacco trade was already very well established. Following the Union of 1707, when the Scots were no longer barred from trading with the English colonies, Glasgow's annual tobacco imports averaged 1.4 million pounds in weight. The golden age of the Scottish trade, from the 1740s to the 1770s, was still to come. In 1771, for example, annual imports had risen dramatically to some 47 million pounds weight.

The Forth & Clyde Canal

Over 90% of the tobacco imported through Port Glasgow and Greenock was re-exported to European markets. The trade, which was firmly in

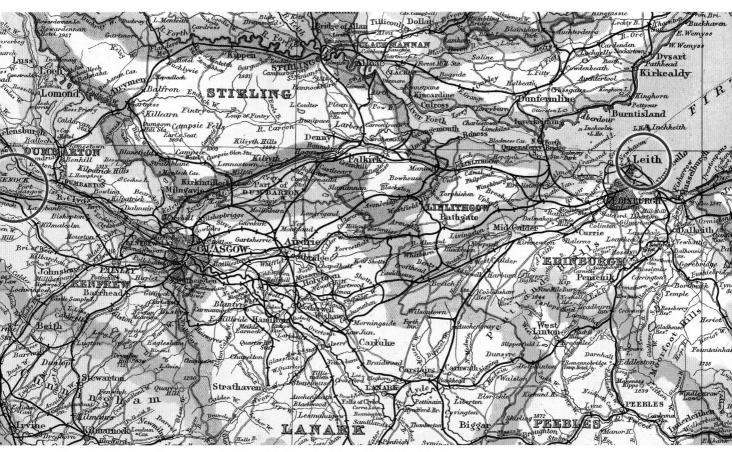

Map showing Port Glasgow on the River Clyde and Leith on the Firth of Forth.
From The Citizen's Atlas of the World, ed. by J G Bartholomew, 1912. Image courtesy of Sheffield University Library.

the grip of the merchants of the City of Glasgow, was transformed by the development of the Clyde into a navigable waterway linked to the Forth and Clyde Canal which was opened in 1790. Largely paid for by the tobacco merchants, the Canal provided a direct and fast link from Glasgow to the major European ports across the North Sea.

Trans-Atlantic trading

The 'tobacco' trade was only one side of what was, in effect, the sale of European goods in American markets in exchange for tobacco, cotton and sugar. To supply stores in Virginia and Maryland, the great Glasgow companies had to secure sources of provisions, ironmongery, textiles and luxury goods. The Glasgow merchants also funded industries such as brewing, linen and coal to ensure cheaper supplies for planter customers in the colonies. The acceleration of the Glasgow tobacco trade has been put down, in part, to smuggling and fraud in the under-weighing of imports. It has been calculated that the Glasgow merchants were paying duty on less than 50% of their imports. But the trade also benefited from the shorter sea routes which were faster, less expensive and safer in times of war than those

A View of Port Glasgow from the South-East

The Tobacco Fleet at anchor at Port Glasgow.
© CSG CIC Glasgow Museums and Libraries Collection: The Mitchell Library.

from Bristol or London, for example. The Glasgow merchants also worked on the basis of quick turn-around times in Virginia, buying crops in advance through local agents rather than waiting in port for consignments.

Bigger, faster ships and a dry dock

By 1775 tobacco firms also owned 90% of the ships. Bigger, faster vessels were designed with more fore-and-aft sails so that they could sail closer to the wind. In 1762 they had the first dry dock in Scotland built so that their ships could be swiftly careened. These larger ships, carrying up to 530,000 pounds, took seven weeks for their outbound trip, with a quick turn-around in Chesapeake Bay and a five-week return journey, a round trip of three months.

Tobacco Lairds, Virginia Dons and Pavement Princes

From 1740 to 1790 almost half of the tobacco merchants were sons or grandsons of established merchants. Through inheritance, the fortunes of an earlier age provided capital for the new era. Under Scottish co-partnership law, only 5% of interest was paid annually to partners, the rest was ploughed back. Those who obtained partnerships dominating the trade were a tiny minority. These wealthy 'Tobacco Lairds', 'Virginia Dons' or 'Pavement Princes', as they were variously called, were an elite within an elite, the majority being sons of well-to-do lowland Scottish families below the level of the aristocracy.

They assumed a distinctive style of dress that made them easily recognizable. Black silk breeches and lavishly trimmed long coats were offset by scarlet cloaks. Accessories included ebony canes with gold or silver handles, tricorn hats and gleaming silver buckles on their shoes. They acquired landed estates as well as smart town houses, spending the working week in the city and the weekends in the country, normally a short horse-ride from Glasgow.

Slave labour

The trans-Atlantic trade made these tobacco merchants some of the richest men in the world. On return journeys their ships were laden not only with tobacco, but also cotton and sugar, all from plantations cultivated by African slaves. Some 30% of the Jamaican sugar plantations were owned by Scots who had a reputation as harsh taskmasters. Life expectancy for a slave there was around four years after arrival. Slavery in Britain was abolished in 1807, as a result of William Wilberforce's campaign. Although Glasgow had a strong abolitionist movement and the owning of personal slaves was banned in Scotland in 1778, almost 30 years before its formal abolition, it has to be said that the wealth of Glasgow and its merchants was inextricably linked to slave labour.

A commanding figure

There are no portraits of Robert Findlay, the Tobacco Merchant, but in the Findlay 'Red Book' he is described as 'a very tall, handsome man, six feet four inches tall or thereabouts and portly

Cartouche from 'A Map of Virginia, drawn by Joshua Fry & Peter Jefferson in 1751'.
Note the central figure in characteristic 'Virginia Don' garb, with scarlet coat and tricorn hat.
© The Library of Virginia.

in proportions'. He was also 'fond of all manner of manly sports and exercises for which Ayrshire used to be, and still is, distinguished'. Having spent those formative four years in Virginia, he had developed a thorough knowledge of the trans-Atlantic trade. He was a very wealthy young man when he and his wife Dorothy bought Easterhill in 1783 and 42 Miller Street a year later.

The American War of Independence

The outbreak of war between the American colonies and Britain in 1775 and the US Declaration of Independence in 1776 posed a potentially mortal threat to the Glasgow tobacco trade. The legal monopoly of British tobacco merchants was destroyed. By 1790 the trade had not reached 25% of pre-war levels. Robert Findlay, however, was one of the few prescient Glasgow merchants who bought up crops in the last months of peace. He shipped them back to Glasgow where he stored them in the Virginia Buildings, newly erected directly behind 42 Miller Street. He waited until prices rose and made a killing. In each corner of the main rooms in the Tobacco Merchant's House, the massive full-height iron doors which protected the safes where the monies and valuable documents associated with the trade were stored, can still be seen today.

Distinguished citizen of Glasgow

Robert Findlay's future prosperity was now assured. He had a wife, a son, three daughters, a country estate and a grand town house. Highly regarded by his fellow merchants, he was Chairman of the Chamber of Commerce from

1789-1794. As Dean of Guild in 1797-98 he was connected to The Merchants House which looked after the poor, the widowed and the orphaned of merchant families.

Glasgow's cultural life

The wealthy Tobacco Lairds sponsored various types of cultural activity in Glasgow. The Hodge Podge Club and the Glasgow Literary Society held debates and discussions. Among the Club's eminent invited speakers was Adam Smith, Glasgow University's Professor of Moral Philosophy. The Tobacco Lairds would become Smith's model of the entrepreneurial businessman with their profits being ploughed back into their businesses under the annual 5% rule, and their commitment to charitable foundations, churches, hospitals and universities. It has to be said, however, that

Watercolour of the Dean of Guild's Medal.
© Glasgow University Library, Special Collections.

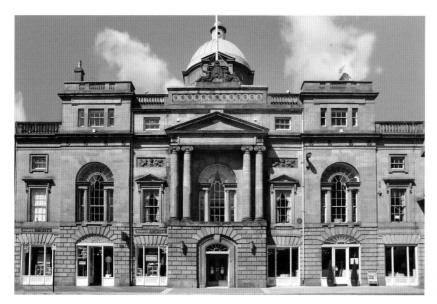

The Trades Hall in Glassford Street, designed by Robert Adam, where the Donaldson Grand Organ was first installed in 1797. © The Trades House of Glasgow.

in the early part of the 18th century, the younger merchants generally preferred hard drinking and tavern gossip to cultural pursuits and intellectual debate.

The Sacred Music Institution

In 1796 Robert Findlay was one of the founding Directors of the Sacred Music Institution in Glasgow, a short-lived music society 'designed to promote a taste in sacred music'. One of the Institution's major projects was the installation in July 1797 of a new 'Donaldson' Grand Organ in the Trades Hall in Glassford Street, designed by architect Robert Adam. After only five years, with the Institution owing unpaid rent arrears to the Trades Hall, the instrument was transferred to Glasgow Cathedral. The Institution finally ceased to exist in 1805.

The builder of the Grand Organ, John Donaldson from York, was the father of John Donaldson, the piano teacher, who went on to marry Robert Findlay's youngest daughter Dorothea, a marriage that was to cause the family so much trouble over the next half-century. The Donaldson Grand Organ is now housed in the organists' training college in Toulouse awaiting refurbishment.

A tragic accident

The life of Robert Findlay, wealthy Tobacco Merchant, commanding Glasgow figure and a man in his prime, was tragically cut short on 31st March 1802 when he was killed in a riding accident. His death was a terrible shock, not only for his widow Dorothy, but for the whole family. Their eldest daughter Janet was to be married the following year to John Bannatyne, her father's managing business partner in London. Their younger daughters Annabella and Dorothea were only fourteen and ten. Their son Robert was just eighteen when he had to carry the full weight of family responsibility.

11. Robert Findlay, 'The Banker'

Young Robert's education

From the time of his father's death, young Robert and his grandfather, Rev Dr Findlay, became very close. His natural bent was towards literature, reflecting his grandfather's academic interests. His school career at Glasgow College had been brilliant, he being the fourth generation of Findlays to have been educated there. The Glasgow University register lists him as graduating with an MA in 1802. It was expected that he would go on to further study at Oxford but on his father's sudden death in March that year, he was destined to join the family business straightaway. He married Mary Buchanan on 23rd April 1810 and they went on to have eleven children.

The sale of 42 Miller Street

In 1818, he decided to sell the house in Miller Street to Findlay, Hopkirk and Company, in which he was a partner. As it was no longer the Findlay family's town house, the Broadwood square piano's new home would probably have been Easterhill, where Dorothea, now aged 26 and the only unmarried member of the family, was still living with her brother Robert, his wife and young family, and their elderly mother.

The Tobacco Merchant's House, 42 Miller Street, in the foreground.

The business in crisis

The family business flourished under young Robert's guidance until 1825 when there was a major financial crisis which swept away many of the oldest and wealthiest 'commercial houses' in the country. What was called 'Sir Robert Peel's Act' decreed the resumption of cash payments in lieu of the depreciated paper money which had come into use during the long Napoleonic Wars. This caused enormous losses to those who had contracted debts in paper and now had to pay them off in gold. The Findlay Bannatyne Company might have weathered the storm as far as their own liabilities were concerned but they were connected to other businesses in even direr straits and wrecked their own fortunes in trying to help save them. To add to his difficulties,

Robert's mother Dorothy Findlay, who bought the Broadwood piano, died at Easterhill in 1829, aged 69.

Family responsibilities and a new career in banking

By 1829 Robert and Mary had had their eleven children, the fifth of whom, Thomas Dunlop Findlay, was later to go into partnership with

Glasgow & Ship Bank £1 note from the 1830s.
© Museum on the Mound, Edinburgh.

my great-grandfather, the shipbuilder Peter Denny. For a man with such a large family the collapse of the business could not have come at a worse time. Relief was to come in 1835 when Robert's old friend James Dennistoun retired from the management of The Glasgow Bank. On Dennistoun's recommendation, with the agreement of the Directors, Robert was appointed as his successor. He had now become 'Robert the Banker'.

Soon after his appointment, the Glasgow Bank took over The Ship Bank, the oldest bank in Glasgow and, under the new name of 'The Glasgow and Ship Bank', it continued to prosper.

However, following a disagreement with the Directors on a matter of moral principle, his connection with that bank ceased in the 1840s. Supported by friends, he established a new bank which then amalgamated with the Union Bank of Scotland.

Photo of Robert Findlay, 'Robert the Banker', in his later years.

Retirement at Boturich

In 1850, now in his sixties, with a reputation for his business skills, urbanity and high moral principles, Robert the Banker retired and moved from Easterhill to Boturich Castle on the shore of Loch Lomond where he spent the rest of his days. Boturich had come into the Findlay family through Robert's wife Mary Buchanan. He had survived the collapse of the business in 1825, turned around his family's fortunes and should have looked forward to a long and happy retirement with Mary at Boturich - but it was not to be.

The Donaldson litigation

When his grandfather Rev Dr Findlay died in 1814, Robert had inherited the role of 'cautioner' for John Bannatyne's tutorship responsibility for his pet sister Dorothea. He thus became directly involved in what became known as 'the Donaldson litigation'. In 1820 Dorothea had married her music teacher, John Donaldson, described in the Red Book as 'a man of considerable accomplishments, although of humble origin, who rose to become Professor of Music at Edinburgh University, and who....was very popular in society.'

Although the family might have got over their concern that Donaldson was not a proper match for her, the course he adopted seems to have precluded that possibility. Having matriculated in law at Oxford in 1823, Donaldson was admitted to the Faculty of Advocates in Edinburgh in June 1826. A year later, in the Court of Session, the newly qualified advocate instituted lawsuits against his brother-in-law Robert Findlay and John Bannatyne, the subject being Dorothea's patrimony.

'A cur and a scoundrel'

According to the Findlay Red Book, the lawsuits were more directed at John Bannatyne but there was really no such distinction as Robert was now also legally involved as cautioner. The family always believed 'they were the acts of a cur and a scoundrel who, having carried off a lady of a family far above anything he had a right to aspire to, took this means of being revenged, because, forsooth, her relations declined to recognize such a dishonourable proceeding'.

Appeals to the House of Lords

Robert the Banker twice appealed the decisions of the Court of Session to the House of Lords; twice they were reversed in his favour. Although Dorothea died as late as 1858, the proceedings were still pending in 1862 when Robert died. Donaldson himself died in 1865. The unresolved case was later quoted in Parliament as a specimen of the law's delays in Scotland. As the Red Book has it: 'Carried on as it was by Donaldson in the most vindictive manner, it was a lifetime persecution (as it was meant to be) to Robert [the Banker]. There is no doubt it was a case trumped up by Donaldson and kept going by Edinburgh lawyers to whom it was as good as an annuity; and so they kept it going until the 1860s'.

'A heavy burden to carry'

At the time of the second appeal to the Lords, Robert was taken ill. It was always believed by the family that anxiety connected with the appeal brought on his fatal illness. On his death bed in 1862, Robert the Banker was heard to say that he had had a heavy burden to carry.

12. 'The Flighty Dorothea' and John Donaldson

Donaldson Senior, the organ builder

Dorothea Findlay's music teacher and future husband, John Donaldson, was christened in Newcastle-upon-Tyne on 5th January 1789 along with two sisters, Elizabeth and Jane, so they may have been triplets born in very late 1788. His father, also John Donaldson, was a well-established organ builder, based in Newcastle from around 1783 until 1790, and then in York until his death in 1807. In 1797, he built one of his most important instruments, the Grand Organ for the Sacred Music Institution in the Trades Hall in Glasgow's Glassford Street. As a Founding Director of the Institution that commissioned the new organ, Dorothea's father, Robert Findlay, the Tobacco Merchant, would have had frequent contact with Donaldson Senior but this would have been to discuss business and musical matters rather than on a social footing.

John Donaldson, music teacher

When his father was installing the Grand Organ in 1797, the young John Donaldson was only eight years old. Although his father had died in 1807, Donaldson maintained his links with Glasgow and in 1811, when he was 23, was listed as a music teacher living at 21 Glassford Street, close to the Trades Hall.

Donaldson, Jas. spirit dealer, 58, Maxwell-street
Donaldson & M'Feat, music-sellers, 50, Glassford-str.
Donaldson, John, professor of music, 3, George's place
Donaldson, C. drawing academy, 136, Trongate
Donaldson, Robert, grocer, 104, High-street
Donaldson & Carruthers, smiths, 34, Main-str. Gorbals

'Donaldson & McFeat, Music Sellers', and 'John Donaldson, Professor of Music', listed in the Glasgow Post Office Directory for 1816.
© National Library of Scotland.

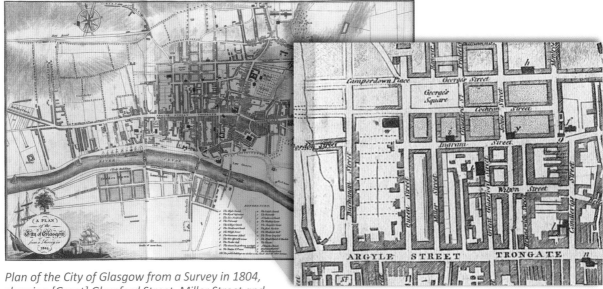

Plan of the City of Glasgow from a Survey in 1804, showing [Great] Glassford Street, Miller Street and George's Square.
© The Mitchell Library, Special Collections.

Dorothea's piano lessons

In 1811, Dorothea Findlay had reached her 19th birthday and was continuing her lessons on the square piano with John Donaldson, whose house in Glassford Street was just two streets away from the Findlays' town house in Miller Street. Doubtless her mother would still have wished Donaldson to come to the house in Miller Street to teach Dorothea on the square piano there but, whether chaperoned or not, it seems clear that Dorothea's relationship with Donaldson was blossoming at this early stage.

By 1816, Donaldson was also listed as having a music shop, trading under the name 'Donaldson & McFeat, Music Sellers', at 50 Glassford Street, close to the Trades Hall and the house he had been living in at number 21. The shop was also a Broadwood agency so it is probable that Donaldson sent a regular tuner round to look after the Findlays' square piano.

'Findlay arrogance, not an unknown commodity'

On their weekly visits to town for Dorothea's music lessons in Miller Street, Mrs Findlay would have had frequent contact with Donaldson, but treating this music teacher and 'mere shopkeeper' as 'in trade' and certainly not as a social equal. This mirrored the earlier relationship between her late husband Robert Findlay, the Tobacco Merchant, and Donaldson's father, the organ builder. Dorothea's mother, her grandfather Rev Dr Findlay and her brother Robert would have shared their concerns about her developing relationship with Donaldson. For his part, Donaldson would have been only too conscious of the Findlays' superior attitude to him.

Johann Bernhard Logier, by Charles Turner, 1819.
© National Portrait Gallery, London.

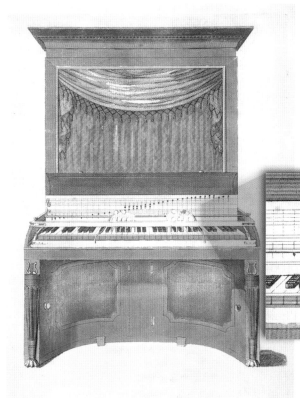

Logier's Chiroplast, from 'The First Companion to the Royal Patent Chiroplast' by JB Logier, 1830.
© Glasgow University Library, Special Collections.

Donaldson and the 'chiroplast'

With his shop well established in 1816, Donaldson had moved out of his house at 21 Glassford Street to No. 3 George's Place, slightly West of George's Square, an address in a smarter part of town. There he gave music classes based on the methods of the Dublin-based German piano teacher and music seller Johann Bernhard Logier whom he had visited in Ireland the year before. It was also in 1816 that he published his 'New System of Musical Tuition as Taught by Mr Donaldson'.

Logier had developed and patented the 'chiroplast' or 'hand-director' mechanism, a transverse frame clamped above the piano keyboard, with two laterally sliding guides resembling 'knuckle-dusters', which held the fingers in the correct position. Although the chiroplast enjoyed considerable success in Britain and Germany it was very controversial and potentially damaging to the hands and wrists. Robert Schumann, for example, is known to have used a chiroplast as a last resort to alleviate his famous hand injury.

The *Cambridge Companion to Schumann* (CUP, 2007), comments: 'that Schumann continues with the chiroplast treatment, even in the face of its dubious effectiveness...shows him...submitting to a slow and thorough-going form of brutality that eventually results in lasting, debilitating injury'.

Donaldson was now also offering *group* piano teaching with the chiroplast at a fee of four guineas per quarter, an innovative (and lucrative) approach to musical tuition. In 1817 Donaldson persuaded Logier to travel from Dublin to Glasgow to conduct a public examination of his pupils in the Assembly Rooms; among them, perhaps, was his pupil Dorothea Findlay, then aged 25. It is not known how many of his pupils suffered debilitating injury from his chiroplast teaching method.

Donaldson marries Dorothea Findlay

According to the Findlay Red Book, Dorothea 'ran away and married her music teacher, John Donaldson' in 1820; by then she was 28, almost 'on the shelf' in those days. Having inherited little from his organ-builder father, Donaldson was determined to secure Dorothea's patrimony before they got married but came up against strong Findlay family opposition. After a long delay and still having failed to achieve a settlement, they were married by Dr Daniel Dewar, Minister of the Tron Kirk, one of the most prestigious churches in Glasgow. Even if the wedding was thinly attended by the Findlay family, it was hardly a case of literally 'running away', perhaps more an act of public defiance.

Donaldson the composer

Around 1822, Donaldson's *Piano Sonata in G Minor* was published in London by Clementi & Co, with a dedication to Muzio Clementi, the renowned Italian composer, pianist, instrument-maker and publisher who spent most of his life in England. It is clear from the dedication that Donaldson now had important musical contacts at the highest national level - and wanted the world to know it. The Sonata has been described by Dr Christopher Field of the University of Edinburgh School of Music as 'one of the most ambitious sonatas by any British native composer of the period'. An original copy held by the British Library has a pencilled note on the front cover: 'To John Shore Esq., with JD's kindest regards'; that John Shore has yet to be identified. A specially commissioned recording of the Sonata, performed by Inja Davidović on a modern Steinway Grand, is included on the CD at the back of this book.

A bitter legal dispute is launched

Donaldson's reputation as musician, teacher and composer was now firmly established. It seems all the stranger, therefore, that after marrying Dorothea in 1820 and publishing his Sonata a year or so later, he changed course and went to Oxford to read Law, matriculating in 1823. However, his choice of topic for his 'Disputatio juridica', or thesis required for admission to the Faculty of Advocates in Edinburgh in 1826, suggests that his decision to read law and his application to the Faculty were strongly influenced by his pursuit of Dorothea's

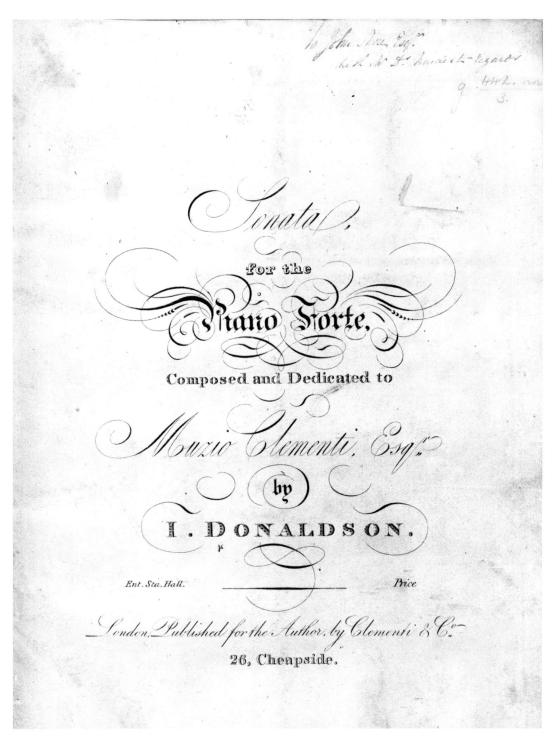

Title page of John Donaldson's Sonata in G Minor, published by Clementi & Co, ca. 1822.
© The British Library Board 2013.

patrimony; his topic, in Latin, was *Si familia furtum fecisse dicatur*, i.e. 'whether members of a family may be said to have committed theft'.

An ambitious man from a relatively humble social background, with a wife from a well-established wealthy family to support, Donaldson needed the money to pursue his career and attain what he saw as their rightful place in society. But Dorothea's patrimony had failed to materialize and the Findlay family held him in disdain. Equipped with his new legal qualification, he was now even more determined to win a satisfactory settlement. In 1827 he launched the bitter legal dispute against Dorothea's brother Robert the Banker and her brother-in-law John Bannatyne that was to last almost half a century. As a qualified lawyer, endowed with a high intelligence and driven by a deep sense of grievance and injustice, he was a formidable, relentless adversary.

In the Findlay Red Book, James Findlay, Robert the Banker's third son (and thus Dorothea's nephew), wrote: 'Carried on as it was by Donaldson in the most vindictive manner, [the litigation] was a lifetime's persecution (as it was intended to be) to my father…for it must be remembered that had Donaldson succeeded in establishing his claim with so many years interest added…it would have been a second ruin to his fortunes. It has always been believed in the family that anxiety connected with it brought on his fatal illness'. Against *this* background, the Findlay family's long-held view that Donaldson was 'a cur and a scoundrel' is, perhaps, not that surprising.

William Sterndale Bennett, engraved by DJ Pound from a photograph by John Mayall.
© National Portrait Gallery, London.

The Edinburgh University Chair of Music

Donaldson's *academic* ambition lay in the field of musical research. In 1838 he applied for a new Chair of Music founded at Edinburgh University with a legacy from a General Reid, but failed to win the post. He applied again in 1841 when the post fell vacant; again he failed. The post fell vacant again in 1844 and Donaldson applied; unable to decide between Donaldson and the Sheffield-born William Sterndale Bennett (who, born in 1816, was 28 years his junior), the University Senatus offered the post to a third candidate who failed to take up the post.

A year later, now aged 57, Donaldson applied for the Chair a *fourth* time, this time successfully. Sterndale Bennett was to go on to an even more prestigious post in due course.

Donaldson's reputation in the field of acoustics

Donaldson immediately set about equipping his University classroom with experimental apparatus. Brought up by his organist father, he had had ample experience of the practical aspects of organ technology but it was in the *scientific* aspects that he was particularly interested. He attached great importance to the teaching of acoustics, a branch of scientific study which, in his own words, 'not only leads to greater excellence in the art itself, but enlarges the understanding, and strengthens the intellectual powers'.

Although he published relatively little on the subject himself, he had established a national reputation in the field. In 1856 for example, Sir William Herschel, the renowned astronomer and Fellow of the Royal Society, urged the University of Cambridge to appoint to the vacant Chair of Music 'a professor able to give lectures in which the principles of the physical science of sound shall be made (as at a scientific university they ought to be) an integral feature - to do, in short, what Donaldson is doing for Edinburgh'.

The Reid Concert Hall

Within a few months of his appointment, furious arguments arose within the University over Donaldson's demands upon the General Reid Bequest to buy more musical apparatus.

Sir William Herschel FRS, by L F Abbott, 1785.
© National Portrait Gallery, London.

The Reid Concert Hall at Edinburgh University.
© Kim Traynor, via Wikimedia Commons.

Donaldson eventually won this battle, resulting in the building of a new Music Class Room, now the Reid Concert Hall. His colleagues must have found it difficult to deal with his obvious ambition, single-mindedness and legalistic demeanour.

The Reid Concert Hall still houses 'The John Donaldson Collection of Musical Instruments' where wind, string and percussion instruments from all over the globe are displayed in what is thought to be the world's oldest purpose-built museum of musical instruments.

St Cecilia's Hall and the Reid Music Library

As an extension of Donaldson's pioneering museum, the University's St Cecilia's Hall, dating from 1763, houses the world famous Russell Collection of early keyboard instruments, many maintained as playing examples. Some 50 of the world's most important, richly decorated and best preserved keyboard instruments from Britain and Europe are housed there. Several playable examples of early Broadwood instruments, including square pianos, are on display. Another less visible achievement was Donaldson's establishment of the Reid Music Library, originally known as The Theory of Music Class Library. From 1859 it was housed in a purpose-built room next to the instrument museum. It was separately managed by the Professor of Music until 1947 when it became the responsibility of the University Library, with a 'Reid Librarian' in charge of it. More recently it was integrated into the University Library's main collections.

Portrait of John Donaldson by William Smellie Watson RSA.
© University of Edinburgh Fine Art Collection.

Donaldson makes his mark in Edinburgh

Five years after his appointment to the Chair, Donaldson's portrait by William Smellie Watson was exhibited at the Royal Scottish Academy in 1849. Here was a very public signal that John Donaldson had made his mark; he was playing a major part in the musical and social life of the University and the City of Edinburgh. Each year he attracted eminent musicians to perform at the annual Reid Concert and in 1860, he gave a banquet in the Corn Exchange to celebrate the completion of the Reid School.

A national figure

Donaldson also involved himself in musical matters at national level: for example, in 1860 he was a member of the Society of Arts Committee on Uniform Musical Pitch. As an acoustics expert, he had much to contribute to the field. The Committee included such other significant national figures as Mr W [Walter Fowler?] Broadwood from the piano company and William Sterndale Bennett, who had been appointed to the Chair of Music at Cambridge in 1856, following Herschel's advice that the University 'look for a man to do, in short, what Donaldson is doing for Edinburgh'. Although Donaldson had attained his Edinburgh Chair some eleven years earlier, the appointment of the much younger Sterndale Bennett to this even more prestigious chair must have grated with Donaldson at Edinburgh.

John and Dorothea Donaldson played a prominent part not only in the social and musical life of Edinburgh but also in London, going to concerts, meeting leading figures in the musical field and attending scientific meetings on acoustics. They enjoyed attending the first Handel Festival at the Crystal Palace in 1857, but just one year later on 11th October 1858, Dorothea died from double pleurisy, aged 66.

The end of the saga

As a widower, John Donaldson lived another seven years, his health declining rapidly. Alone and embittered, without having ever received what he believed was due to him, he carried on his fruitless litigation until the day he died at home of inflammation of the bladder, on 12th August 1865. All the other parties to the case had died some years before. The Findlay family had held him responsible for causing Robert the Banker's untimely death through stress and anxiety and despised him for it. The only winners were the lawyers. In the words of the House of Lords Tribunal report on the case, dated 20th July 1864: 'It is very distressing to any tribunal to find itself called upon to sit in judgement on matters of account now above half-a-century old, long after all the parties connected with them have been in their graves'.

An obituary in the *Edinburgh Evening Courant* showed a rather different side to Donaldson's nature: 'By all who knew him, Mr Donaldson's loss will be deeply lamented. His gentle, sensitive spirit shrank from the discords of public life, and his fastidious taste debarred him from all rude enjoyments. But he was tenderly loved by all those who knew and understood him, and warmly loved by all who sympathised with his thoroughly musical nature'. These sentiments were certainly not shared by the Findlay family and the writer's observation that 'his gentle, sensitive spirit shrank from the discords of public life' doesn't exactly square with Donaldson's fierce, lifelong litigation against them.

It was a sad end to an otherwise highly distinguished academic and gifted musical career.

John Donaldson had met Dorothea Findlay over the keys of the Broadwood square piano. Childless,

St John's Episcopal Church, Edinburgh, where John and Dorothea Donaldson are buried. © Paul Boxley, via Wikimedia Commons.

they lie buried at St John's Episcopal Church in Edinburgh. The piano lived on to tell their story.

Postscript: 'Jarndyce v Jarndyce'

There is a remarkable parallel between the Donaldson legal dispute and the long-running *Jarndyce v Jarndyce* Court of Chancery case in Charles Dickens' novel *Bleak House*. That case, which revolved around a testator who apparently had made several wills, had taken years and incurred court costs of £60,000 to £70,000 [*ca.* £5 million at 2013 prices]. Dickens had drawn on his own experience as a law clerk and partly as a Chancery litigant himself seeking to enforce copyright on his earlier works. Although the novel was *published* in 1852-53, the English legal historian Sir William Holdsworth set the *action* of the case in 1827, the very year in which John Donaldson launched his litigation. Might Dickens have drawn, in part, from reports of the Donaldson litigation which had already been in train for some 25 years when he wrote the novel?

13. The Irrawaddy Flotilla

TD Findlay and Peter Denny in partnership

It was through my internet search for information about Mrs Findlay, the original owner of the Broadwood square piano, that Robert Findlay's interview with Sarah Powell for *Burke's Peerage and Gentry* had come to light. In the transcript, Robert Findlay had revealed the first of the extraordinary connections between Mrs Findlay's descendents and my mother's Denny forebears: this was the Irrawaddy Flotilla partnership between TD Findlay, one of Mrs Findlay's grandsons, and the Dumbarton shipbuilder Peter Denny, my great-grandfather.

'The Road to Mandalay'

'By the old Moulmein Pagoda, lookin'
eastward to the sea,

There's a Burma girl a-settin' an' I know
she thinks of me...

Come you back to Mandalay, where the
old Flotilla lay:

Can't you 'ear their paddles clunkin' from
Rangoon to Mandalay?'

In these lines from *The Road to Mandalay*, Rudyard Kipling immortalized the Irrawaddy Flotilla. Although he wrote them on the strength of having spent only three days in Burma in 1889, he perfectly captured the nostalgia and longing of

Rudyard Kipling, by Sir Philip Burne-Jones, 2nd Bt.
© National Portrait Gallery, London.

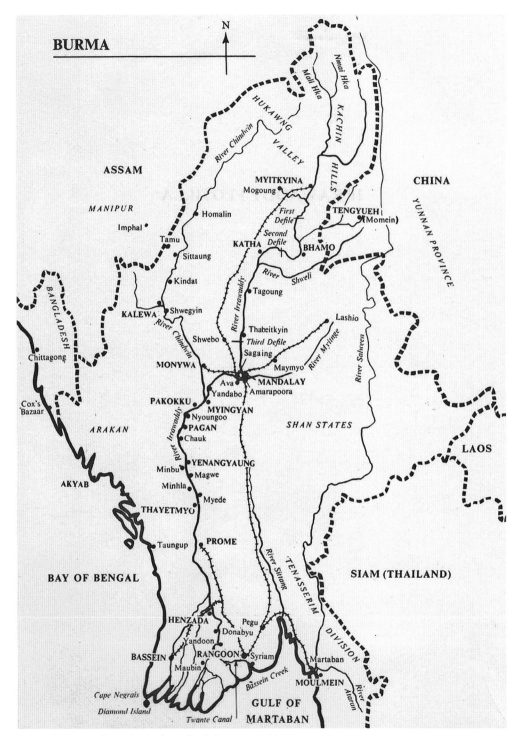

Map of Burma showing the length of the Irrawaddy River.
From 'Irrawaddy Flotilla' by Alister McCrae and Alan Prentice. (Paisley: James Paton, 1978).

'The Old Moulmein Pagoda, lookin' eastward to the sea'. Photograph taken by Bourne & Shepherd in 1870. © British Library Board, 2013.

a British soldier for the exotic delights of Burma and the countries East of Suez. Set to music in 1907 by the American composer Oley Speaks (1874 - 1948), the song was popularized by the Australian bass-baritone Peter Dawson in the 1950s; it remains a popular classic with a rousing chorus.

Coincidentally, Kipling also makes amusing mention of Broadwood pianos in the opening verse of his 1894 *Song of the Banjo:*

'You can't pack a Broadwood half a mile -

You mustn't leave a fiddle in the damp -

You couldn't raft an organ up the Nile,

And play it in an Equatorial swamp.

I travel with the cooking pots and pails -

I'm sandwiched 'tween the coffee and the pork -

And when the dusty column checks and tails,

You should hear me spear the rear-guard to a walk!'

Irrawaddy Steamship, painted by JC Burnie, ca. 1961.
© British Library Board, 2013.

The first Irrawaddy Flotilla

The origins of the Irrawaddy Flotilla lie in the Second Burmese War of 1852. The Governor-General of India, Lord Dalhousie, had visited Rangoon in July 1852 and discovered that there was a serious communication problem with the new frontier station of Thayetmyo, 300 miles up the Irrawaddy River. He ordered a small flotilla of four paddle steamers and four barges, known as 'flats' which were either towed behind or lashed alongside the steamers, to be sent over to Burma from the flotillas of the Bengal Marine. It was this small collection of vessels that formed the original government-owned Irrawaddy Flotilla. Manned by British officers and engineers with ratings from the Chittagong District, this flotilla maintained the link with Thayetmyo for 12 years. By that time, the new Province of British Burma had been created, leaving Upper Burma, rich in natural resources, landlocked and ruled by King Mindon.

The Flotilla is sold to private enterprise

The Chief Commissioner of British Burma saw that trade with Upper Burma could only flourish if the Irrawaddy had a much larger fleet of steam-powered boats funded and run by private enterprise. In 1864 the Irrawaddy Flotilla was sold to the Glasgow firm of teak and rice merchants, Todd, Findlay and Company. Its Chairman, Thomas Dunlop (TD) Findlay, was Robert the Banker's fifth son, thus one of Mrs Findlay's many grandchildren and also Robert and Bill Findlay's great-grandfather.

A syndicate is formed

As extra capital was urgently needed to build new vessels required for the Flotilla, TD Findlay approached two other potential investors: Patrick Henderson & Company, the Glasgow ship-owners, known in their day as 'Paddy Henderson', who traded to Burma, and the Dumbarton shipbuilder Peter Denny, my great-grandfather. The three parties formed a syndicate to take over the Irrawaddy Flotilla and the contract to operate it through floating a new public company.

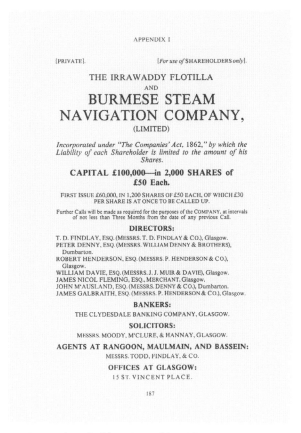

Notice to Shareholders, issued in 1864.
From 'Irrawaddy Flotilla' by Alister McCrae and Alan Prentice.

Boats of the Flotilla Company.
© The Kipling Society.

A new company takes over

In December 1864, a Notice to Shareholders was issued by this new company, 'The Irrawaddy Flotilla and Burmese Steam Navigation Company Limited'. It announced that it would take over the Government vessels and the operating contract on 1st January 1865.

New paddle-steamers and flats were designed in Peter Denny's yard in Dumbarton as flat-bottomed

The Irrawaddy Flotilla Company 1865 company emblem.
© Scottish Maritime Museum.

vessels able to navigate the shallow waters of the Irrawaddy. Prefabricated in his and other Clyde yards, they were shipped out to Burma and reassembled there. The new company flourished, ploughing back profits into new steamers and flats and sending out British officers to man the growing fleet.

The Irrawaddy Flotilla Company Limited

The Directors in Glasgow quickly developed an expansion plan which needed further capital investment. By 1875 the fleet comprised 10 paddle-steamers and 16 flats, with none of the original Government vessels remaining. The

The Fleet mustering for advance on Mandalay, line drawing by J C Burnie. From 'Irrawaddy Flotilla' by Alister McCrae and Alan Prentice.

prospectus drew attention to 'the potential for future trading and monopolizing the river trade, previously conducted by an estimated 25,000 native country boats; the fleet now navigates the Irrawaddy for 1,000 miles, from Rangoon to Bhamo, close to the frontier with China and a great depot of trade with Yunan conveyed by trains of mule caravans'. Under a new agreement with King Mindon, the steamer service had been extended to Mandalay, the new capital of Upper Burma, and from there on to Bhamo. From January 1876

the company changed its name to 'The Irrawaddy Flotilla Company Limited'.

An ultimatum to the new King

After King Mindon died in 1878, there was political turmoil in Upper Burma. Although the Flotilla maintained good relations with his successor, King Thebaw, increasing lawlessness was causing severe problems for trade on the Irrawaddy. The Commissioner issued an ultimatum to the King requiring him to submit to several unconditional proposals which directly threatened his independence. The dangerous task of delivering the ultimatum was assigned to one of the Flotilla Company's senior Captains, who awaited the King's reply for a week at Mandalay before receiving his refusal to concede. The Company then embarked a force of 10,000 soldiers, 7,000 camp followers, 500 mules and two mountain batteries of artillery. They were taken up the river and after a short engagement with Burmese forces, Mandalay was easily taken. The last King of Burma and his Queen were taken away on the Company's steamer *Thooreah* to Rangoon. From there they went into exile in India. It would take

another five years for peace to be restored to Upper Burma.

In 1884, following the death of James Galbraith (one of the original Directors), Peter Denny, who was Chairman, also took over as Managing Director of the Flotilla Company. He carried on both these offices for ten years, while still remaining the leading figure in the Denny shipbuilding firm in Dumbarton.

Peter Denny maintained the ambitious policies for the Flotilla which he and Galbraith had adopted from the start. These policies were to be carried forward by other members of the Denny family in future years.

By 1888 the fleet had rapidly expanded to 81 steamers and over 100 flats. Of the steamers, 20

Peter Denny, the author's great-grandfather; portrait by Daniel Macnee, RSA, 1868.
© National Maritime Museum.

Elephants stacking teak in TD Findlay & Son's yard in Moulmein.
From 'Irrawaddy Flotilla' by Alister McCrae and Alan Prentice.

were screw-driven, a design more practical than paddlewheels for the waters of the Irrawaddy Delta. The main Irrawaddy trade was in rice and teak. The rice was taken downstream in flats to Moulmein for export worldwide. The teak trees were felled after 'ringing' to let them dry out on the stump for a few years. To ensure future supplies, for every tree felled, the Flotilla Company planted five saplings, an early example of 'sustainable forestry'. Several hundred contractors' elephants then dragged the logs to the nearest floating stream to await the rains which would carry them to the main river. Here they were turned into rafts large enough to carry a whole family downstream to the base at Moulmein where the logs were sawn into saleable products and exported.

La Platense Flotilla Company

By 1889 the Directors of the Flotilla Company were proclaiming that 'there is no such river fleet in the world'. In an attempt to repeat their success on the Irrawaddy, the Denny and Henderson families had taken a major share in the La Platense Flotilla Company in 1882 to operate river steamers in Argentina and Uruguay. This venture was plagued with difficulty and faced strong local competition. Peter Denny's eldest son, William, a brilliant engineer who was playing a key role in the design of new ships, went out to join the La Platense Company Board and save the business from catastrophe. He recommended that they should buy out the local competition but this led to colossal financial loss, leaving both parent companies with massive debts to write off.

William Denny 1847-1887, etching by Jules Jacquet, frontispiece to 'The Life of William Denny', by Alexander Bruce (London: Hodder & Stoughton, 1888).

William Denny's death in Buenos Aires

Before leaving for South America, William had suffered from ill health and his home had been destroyed in a fire. Plagued with guilt at his failure to save the business and missing his wife and family, he fell into deep depression; on 17th March 1887, aged only 39, he committed suicide in Buenos Aires. His father, Peter Denny, was hit very hard by this devastating blow and, aged 66, virtually retired from the business.

The inter-War years

Between the two World Wars the Irrawaddy Flotilla had grown enormously to some 650 vessels, with 300 steamers and five dockyards at Rangoon, Mandalay and Moulmein. In its prime, it directly employed over 12,000 people with thousands more linked to the trade the length of the Irrawaddy.

The end of an era

When the Japanese invaded Burma in 1941-42 the British forces fell back to India. Most of the Company's fleet were systematically scuttled to prevent them falling into Japanese hands.

Even after Burma was taken back in 1945, the Irrawaddy Flotilla Company never really recovered. River services were carried on by the Government Inland Water Transport Board, still in the old Flotilla livery, but they never matched its pre-war scale. The Findlay teak business paid off its employees and dispensed with the elephants in 1945. The family tried briefly to build up the Burma business again only to see it nationalized by the independent Burmese government in 1948.

It was the dynamic partnership between Mrs Findlay's grandson TD Findlay and my great-grandfather Peter Denny that lay behind the dramatic growth and success of the magnificent Irrawaddy Flotilla Company. Its glory days were now over.

Denial to the Japanese invader - the fleet is scuttled; line drawing by JC Burnie.
From 'Irrawaddy Flotilla' by Alister McCrae and Alan Prentice.

14. The Dennys of Dumbarton

The Denny Brothers partnership

The Denny shipbuilding tradition goes back to William Denny I, 'William of the Woodyard' (1779-1833), who started building wooden sailing boats in Dumbarton on the River Leven which flows south from Loch Lomond into the Clyde.

William Denny of the Woodyard (1779-1833), by unknown artist.
© Scottish Maritime Museum

After his death, three of his six sons, William Denny ll (b.1815), Alexander (b. 1818) and Peter (b. 1821), set up a partnership of marine architects in 1844, known as 'Denny Brothers', to design iron steamships. William had been chief draughtsman in the yard of Coats & Young in Belfast, already well-established as an important centre of shipbuilding. Alexander had been in business independently as a marine architect and Peter had been apprenticed first to a local lawyer, then at the glassworks in Dumbarton. Peter went on to become an assistant to his older brother William, who by that stage was yard manager at Robert Napier's yard in Govan, and later worked as an assistant to his other brother Alexander.

William Denny and Brothers

A year after establishing Denny Brothers they set up as shipbuilders in the small Kirk Yard on the River Leven. They then took over the Woodyard where their father had been in business and started building iron steamships, with a labour force of just 14 men. A year later Alexander left to set up his own business and their other older brother James (b.1807) joined the partnership, the company changing its name to 'William Denny and Brothers'.

'William Denny & Brothers Limited' company seal.
© Scottish Maritime Museum.

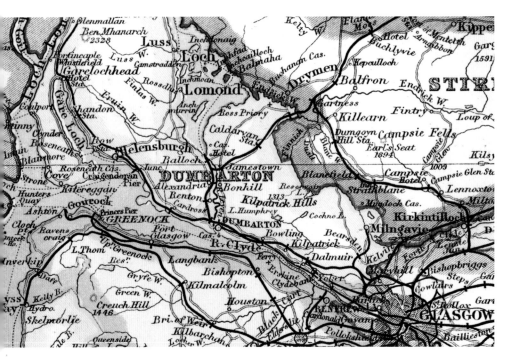

Map showing Glasgow, Dumbarton, Loch Lomond and Rivers Clyde and Leven. From The Citizen's Atlas of the World, ed. by JG Bartholomew, 1912. Image courtesy of Sheffield University Library.

Tulloch & Denny

In 1850, by agreement with William and James, Peter Denny set up a separate marine engineering company, 'Tulloch & Denny', to fit out the hulls that the family partnership were building. Only four years later in 1854, William, the eldest of the brothers, died in 1854 at the early age of 39; this family tragedy marked a turning point in the life of Peter Denny, businessman and entrepreneur.

Peter Denny invests in shipping

As his other brother James began gradually to withdraw from the company, Peter Denny was freer to set new strategic directions and saw fresh opportunities for their shipbuilding business by investing in shipping companies. Through his connections with the Free Church of Scotland he had useful contact with the partners in the Paddy Henderson company and built ships for them. He also joined with their partners speculating in Confederate Bonds and building a blockade runner used by the Confederate navy. This was to evade the Union blockade by trading with Britain and Europe via the West Indies during the American Civil War.

It was also through the Paddy Henderson connection that Peter Denny became a major investor in their New Zealand shipping operations, operated by the Albion Shipping Company. As mentioned previously, in 1864 he was joined by TD Findlay (Mrs Findlay's grandson) and the Henderson partners in establishing the Irrawaddy Flotilla and Burmese Steam Navigation Company.

William Denny III, 1847-87, posthumous portrait painted in 1888 by Norman Macbeth RSA.
© National Maritime Museum.

Peter Denny's son William joins the Company

In Dumbarton, Peter Denny's shipbuilding business had grown dramatically, not least through the building of new vessels for the Flotilla. In 1868 he transferred the whole business to a new purpose-built yard on the River Leven. Three years later he took his eldest son William Denny III into partnership.

William was a gifted experimental scientist who also brought innovative methods of working to the yard. He introduced standardized speed trials over a measured mile for all Denny vessels. This led to the development of new hull designs, including the shallow draught vessels for the Irrawaddy Flotilla. He also pioneered the construction of double cellular bottoms for cargo ships and adopted mild steel instead of iron in ship construction.

The Denny Ship Model Experimental Tank

As part of major developments to the yard, William and his father built the world's first commercial test tank in Dumbarton. The Denny Ship Model Experimental Tank measured 300 ft long by 22 ft wide and 9 ft deep. Trial hull designs, carved in solid paraffin wax, were pulled along in the water by an overhead trolley, the drag being measured by a spring device. In 1888, the Tank enabled the yard to complete the *PS Princess Henriette* for the Belgian Government as the fastest ship in the world, except for naval torpedo boats, at 21 knots. It also turned out to be a vital element in the company's research and development programme throughout its future years. Equally important was the income it attracted from other yards and shipping companies. It is said that every testing tank in the world subsequently built has been 'christened' with a phial of Denny Tank water.

The Denny Experimental Tank in the 1950s.
© Scottish Maritime Museum.

New working practices

William introduced the piece-work system for all the trades in the yard and set up an innovative workers' suggestion scheme, with awards for the best ideas. He also established a works council in 1884 to settle demarcation disputes and discuss charitable giving; remarkably, the rules also applied to the management and stipulated that all fines imposed when rules were broken would be returned to the workforce.

William's death

William's tragic suicide in Buenos Aires in 1887 brought an end to what promised to be a brilliant career. Peter Denny never really recovered from the devastating blow of losing his eldest son at such an early age. He died on 22nd August 1895, aged 73, leaving an estate approaching £200,000, or some £20 million at 2013 prices. It has been estimated that he was among the richest men to die leaving property in Scotland in that year. He had been the major driving force behind the dramatic rise of William Denny and Brothers from its modest beginnings with a workforce of 14 men in 1846 to its becoming one of the world's most innovative and best known shipyards. Highly regarded by his peers, he had been President of the Institute of Marine Engineers and a Vice-President of the Institution of Naval Architects.

Peter Denny, family man

Peter Denny married Helen Leslie on 26th January 1846. They had thirteen surviving children, the youngest of these being my grandfather, Leslie

'Helenslee', aerial photo of Peter Denny's magnificent mansion.
© RCAHMS

Denny (1871-1938). Between 1866 and 1868 Peter Denny built the magnificent mansion 'Helenslee', named in honour of his wife Helen, on a 43-acre site on the north shore of the Clyde, at the huge cost of £10,000.

Philanthropist

Peter Denny was deeply committed to the people of Dumbarton. He funded the building of houses for his workers and gave large sums to charitable bodies such as the Glasgow Western Infirmary. He established scholarships in Dumbarton Schools and the University of Glasgow which, in 1890, awarded him the honorary degree of Doctor of Laws for his services to education. A statue of Peter Denny stands outside the Dumbarton Municipal Buildings, bearing the inscription: 'Erected by friends and fellow townsmen in 1902'. It shows him holding the bow section of a ship in

Peter Denny's statue outside Dumbarton Municipal Buildings. Plaque from the base of Peter Denny's statue showing a propeller being fitted.

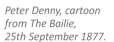

Peter Denny, cartoon from The Bailie, 25th September 1877.

Photograph of Peter Denny. © Scottish Maritime Museum.

one hand and a ship's plan in the other. One of the bronze plaques on the pedestal shows a propeller being fitted to the port side of the rudder on a steel ship, underneath a beautiful scrolled decoration on the taffrail above.

Citizen of Glasgow

Glasgow's pride in Peter Denny was wittily captured in *The Bailie* for Wednesday 25th September 1877. This gossipy paper, published weekly, was the city's premier social periodical from 1872. Peter Denny featured in issue number 255 in the 'Men you Know' column on the front page, accompanied by a finely drawn cartoon of the splendidly bearded shipbuilder, shown against the background of his shipyard and the Rock of Dumbarton.

'More than a mere shipbuilder'

The piece refers to a meeting in Glasgow's Corporation Galleries of the Institution of Naval Architects, its first visit to the city. It described how all the 'strangers' were delighted at the warm Glasgow hospitality and goes on to say: 'of all the bald-headed shell-backs [old sailors] who met last week to chat over the mysteries of naval architecture, not one was more worthy of mention than Peter Denny of Dumbarton…[He] was the equal of them all as a shipbuilder, and was, besides, a man of eager, determined nature, and of a great public spirit…Mr Denny is more than a mere shipbuilder. For years he took a warm interest in the affairs of Dumbarton. Indeed, it would not be too much to say that he was then the biggest man in the burgh. He was Provost from 1851 to 1854. About the latter year he built a handsome and commodious school-house in College Street, for the gratis teaching of the rivet-boys in his employment and this he maintained

Cutty Sark, painted by Frederick Tudgay.
Courtesy of the Cutty Sark Trust, London.

until the Education Act came into operation, solely at his own expense'. The affectionate, witty piece ends with a reference to Noah as 'the first Precedent of the Naval Ark-itects'.

'Cutty Sark'

In addition to the many vessels they built for the Irrawaddy Flotilla, William Denny and Brothers are particularly remembered for three extraordinary ships built under Peter Denny's chairmanship. In 1870, as guarantors, the company took over the contract for the *Cutty Sark* from Scott and Linton who went bankrupt owing to the low contract price. The hull was towed across the river to Dennys' Leven yard, fitted out and rigged ready to sail in just twelve weeks. This historic ship, now a superbly restored national treasure, lies in dry dock at Greenwich, where little mention is made of the crucial role played by Dennys in completing her so quickly.

SS Coya being built on the shore of Lake Titicaca.
© Scottish Maritime Museum.

SS Rotomahana, 'Greyhound of the Pacific'.
© State Library of Victoria, Green Collection.

'SS Rotomahana'

In 1879, following William's pioneering development work in steel shipbuilding, they built the 1,727 ton *Rotomahana,* for the Union Steam Ship Company of New Zealand. This 15.5 knot vessel, dubbed 'Greyhound of the Pacific', was the first seagoing passenger ship built of mild steel and the first fitted with bilge keels for extra stability. During a voyage in January 1880 to show her off at various ports, she touched a rock off the Great Barrier Reef. One plate was dented and a few rivets loosened. Had she been made of iron she would have been a total loss. She was out of service for only 72 hours.

SS Coya in service on Lake Titicaca.
© Graham Lappin Collection.

'SS Coya'

One of their most remarkable achievements was the building of the *SS Coya*, an iron-hulled steamship, for Lake Titicaca in the Andes, at 12,500 ft the highest navigable lake in the world. Drawing on their long Flotilla experience they built the *SS Coya* in knock-down form. They assembled her with nuts and bolts in their Leven yard to check that everything fitted, dismantled her and then shipped her out in thousands of parts small enough to transport by mule up to the lake where she was reassembled with rivets and launched in 1893. She was operated by the Peruvian Corporation, a UK-owned company that had taken over Peru's railways and lake shipping in 1890. At 540 tons and 170 ft long, she was the largest steamship on the lake. She was in service until 1984 when she was grounded after a flood, but in 2001 she was rescued, restored and refloated as a restaurant.

Close-up of the Denny Mumford helicopter with engine and pilot on board. © Scottish Maritime Museum.

The Denny Mumford helicopter. © Scottish Maritime Museum.

The new century

After Peter Denny's death in 1895, his fifth son Archibald took over the direction of the company. The early years of the new century saw the construction of many cross-channel ferries and large refrigerated ships for New Zealand and Spanish lines. It was around this time that my grandfather Leslie Denny had been a Director with a special interest in the development of marine engines, ship stability and paddle wheel design. The company also continued its tradition of innovation through its pioneering work on the helicopter.

The Denny-Mumford helicopter

One of the company's most strikingly innovative projects was the Denny-Mumford helicopter designed by Experimental Tank Superintendent Edwin Mumford and his Chief Assistant, J Pollock Brown, who started experiments using propellers to lift a machine into the air. They experimented with model screw propellers under water and adapted the results to see how a machine would work in the air. Their prototype had a bamboo framework with six large horizontally-mounted fabric propellers, driven by chains and extension shafts, with control from a rudder. The first flight attempts in 1908 failed as the engine was too heavy and the frame too flimsy.

A more powerful engine was added to a new aluminium frame and the machine rose under its own power on 7th September 1912. Unlike current helicopters, it would 'auto-rotate' to a safe landing if the engine failed, which it often did. A final version fitted with floats was successfully tested on the River Clyde; it flew 100 yards at a height of 10 feet but was later destroyed in a gale. The outbreak of war in 1914 put a stop to further developments. Denny innovation had produced what has been described as the world's first helicopter to leave the ground under its own power.

Sir Thomas Lipton and the America's Cup

The company's experience in testing model hulls attracted the attention of Sir Thomas Lipton (1848-1931), the wealthy tea merchant. In his quest for winning the America's Cup he commissioned Dennys to build two of his five 'Shamrock' yachts. He challenged the American holders with five different Shamrocks between 1899 and 1930. Reflecting his Ulster roots, he issued his challenges through the Royal Ulster Yacht Club - as a self-made man he had had to wait until the year before his death to be admitted to the socially exclusive Royal Yacht Squadron. The first of his two Denny Shamrocks had hull frames of manganese bronze with light nickel steel plating, another first in ship construction. He never won the Cup but the Americans presented him with an 18-carat gold cup for 'the best of all losers'.

The First World War

In 1913 Archibald Denny was created 1st Baronet of Dumbarton, reflecting his work on the Safety of Life at Sea (SOLAS) enquiries following the loss of *Titanic*, the company's importance to national defence, its worldwide reputation for shipbuilding and, not least, his father Peter's legacy. From 1905 Dennys had diversified into other specialist areas, including work for the Admiralty. Their defence work included contracts for torpedo boats, destroyers and submarines; they even assembled 150 fighter aircraft.

Sir Thomas Lipton's Shamrock built by Dennys.
© Scottish Maritime Museum.

The inter-War years

Conditions were difficult after the First World War, with shortages of steel, over-capacity in world shipping and growing overseas competition. The company concentrated on the development of high-pressure turbines, hull shapes and stabilizing systems. 'Denny-Brown' stabilizers, developed in collaboration with Brown Bros of Edinburgh, were fitted to warships during the Second World War to provide a more stable platform for their guns. After the War they were used for passenger ships and, now highly developed, are still used throughout the shipping world.

The Second World War

Sir Maurice Denny succeeded his father Archibald in 1936 and oversaw the company going public in 1939. The yard's main output was in warships and merchant vessels, producing twelve destroyers, twelve sloops, two minesweepers, two gunboats, a tank transporter ferry, two merchant aircraft carriers and an aircraft transport ship.

The post-War years

After the war, with the end of the Irrawaddy Flotilla, Dennys stopped making shallow draft vessels. They maintained their market position by building deep-sea merchant ships, short-sea and larger ferries, and smaller craft for the Royal Navy.

The Experimental Tank was also regularly used on a commercial basis by other companies testing new hull designs. The Belfast firm of Harland & Wolff, for example, decided to fit a bulbous bow on the liner *Canberra* after testing models in the tank. After acquisition by Vickers Ltd in 1964, the tank became a branch of the Scottish Maritime Museum in 1982.

Edward Denny becomes Chairman

Edward Denny, my uncle, had become Chairman of the company in 1953 and was to see it through challenging times. In January that year, the Denny-built *Princess Victoria* was lost on the Stranraer-

Dennys' shipyard in the 1950s.
© Scottish Maritime Museum.

Edward Denny, the author's uncle.
Photo courtesy of Dumbarton
Library Heritage Centre.

The Denny Hoverbus, D2-002, on trials.
© Scottish Maritime Museum.

Larne crossing during the European windstorm of 1953; this was due, in part, to the specially fitted 'guillotine door' that would have offered the stern doors greater protection from the waves, not having been deployed before leaving port. This was the worst maritime disaster since the Second World War and a severe blow to the company's prestige. It was a traumatic time for Edward Denny.

The Denny Hoverbus

With increasing competition from Japanese and German yards in the 1950s, the company looked for new products and turned to hovercraft design. Edward Denny stood down as Chairman of the parent company in 1960, and a new subsidiary company, Denny Hovercraft Ltd, was formed to take these developments forward. A full-sized version, the D2-002, was launched in 1962. It carried 88 passengers at up to 25 knots powered by 800bhp engines. After test runs on the Clyde,

the *Denny Hoverbus* made the 820 mile journey from Dumbarton around the north of Scotland to London where it was demonstrated on the Thames. Newsreel film of the time shows passengers being invited to try this novel type of transport at £1 a trip. Despite the early promise, serious problems arose when the underwater propellers and the side-walls or 'skirts' were damaged by river debris. The Denny Hoverbus was the last major project of the parent company before, like many other yards, it went into voluntary liquidation in 1963. During its remarkable history the company had built over 1,500 vessels.

Edward Denny's life in shipbuilding

Born in Dumbarton in 1906, Edward Denny attended schools in Edinburgh, England and Switzerland. While serving his apprenticeship at the company's engine works he studied for his Bachelor of Science degree at Glasgow University.

After working with other companies he joined the company as technical assistant to the General Manager in 1932. He joined the Board in 1943 and, as Chairman ten years later, headed the family firm which had operated for over a century and employed thousands of local people. In his time, he had been an early member of the Council of Industrial Design and, following in his grandfather Peter's footsteps, had been President of the Institute of Marine Engineers.

Edward Denny's life in retirement - new links to the Findlay family

After retirement in 1960, Edward Denny sold his house 'Auchenlinnhe' to Bill and Delia Findlay, another remarkable connection between the two families brought to light through Dorothy Findlay's original purchase of the square piano in 1804 and my mother's buying it at auction in Ballycastle in 1977.

Edward Denny moved to a smaller house at Gartochraggan near Loch Lomond. He took a great interest in conservation and planning, chairing the planning committee of the old Dunbartonshire County Council, where he represented Kilmaranock, his local parish. He became closely involved in the development of the Scottish Maritime Museum and was a regular visitor to its Dumbarton branch, the Denny Ship Model Experimental Tank.

The end of an era

Edward Denny died in 1992, just a year after his older sister Hilda (my mother) died in 1991. Little did they know how her whimsical purchase of the square piano in Ballycastle in 1977 would eventually reveal the extraordinary connections between the Denny and Findlay families. How they would have enjoyed the tale.

PS Lochlomond, or 'Yard No 1', passing Dumbarton Rock, painted by J. Livingstone, 1847. Launched on 16th May 1845, she was the first vessel to leave William Denny & Brothers' yard in Dumbarton. © Scottish Maritime Museum.

15. The Missing Years, 1804 - 1949

The square piano's journey to Ireland

The original Broadwood ledger entry recording Mrs Findlay's purchase of the square piano on Friday 10th August 1804 was the starting point for this book. Without this vital evidence, the extraordinary links between the Findlays and the Dennys, and the romantic saga of 'The Flighty Dorothea' and John Donaldson, would not have come to light.

We know that a month after Mrs Findlay had had the piano delivered 'on hire or purchase' to her daughter Janet's house in London on 10th July 1804, it was taken back to the Broadwood works for packing into its special sea-going crate. It was then taken to Captain Wilson on the *Eliza* for delivery to Mrs Findlay's townhouse at 42 Miller Street in Glasgow. Some 170 years later, my mother bought the piano through PJ McIlroy's auction room in Ballycastle, but there was no evidence of what had happened to the piano between these dates.

Where had the square piano been?

When I first contacted Robert and Bill Findlay, neither of them remembered the piano from their childhood days at Boturich Castle, so it seemed that it had not been in their immediate family for at least the previous two generations. I next contacted the auctioneer PJ McIlroy's son Sean, who had succeeded his late father in running the family business in Ballycastle, to find out if he had any record of who had put the piano into the auction in 1977.

Sean McIlroy had known my mother and, crucially, remembered that as a young man he had helped his father carry the piano into the auction room. Although he couldn't trace the auction record for the sale, he thought the vendor was a Robin Walsh who lived in Cushendun, a small town on the Antrim coast some twelve miles south of Ballycastle.

Sean McIlroy in his Ballycastle office,
holding the name board of the square piano.
A portrait of his father 'PJ' hangs on the wall.
Reproduced with Sean McIlroy's kind permission.

The piano moves from Belfast to Cushendun

I contacted a 'Robin Walsh' listed in the telephone directory as living in Cushendun and it was he who had put the piano into the Ballycastle auction. Now in his 80s, he was surprised to be reacquainted with the piano and delighted to hear about its original owner. He had bought it in a Belfast auction in 1949, shortly before he and his wife Rosemary were married in April that year. They needed a large piece of furniture for the sitting room in their first flat in Belfast and thought the piano was an interesting instrument which he could try to restore. He remembered paying £7-10s-0d for it, including a ten shilling tip to the porter who had done the bidding for him, but he couldn't recall which auction house he had bought it at. He sent me a black and white photograph he had taken of it in their flat in 1949.

The Broadwood square piano in Robin Walsh's flat in Belfast in April 1949.
Photo by courtesy of Robin Walsh.

Robin Walsh still had some new piano wire given to him by a contact at Crymble's Music Shop in Belfast who had volunteered to help him with the restringing. Sadly, his contact had died and the restoration never went ahead. When he retired in 1977, Robin and Rosemary Walsh moved from Belfast to their holiday home in Cushendun and, having no space for the piano, put it into the nearest auction in Ballycastle.

Robin Walsh, holding the name board of the square piano at his home in Cushendun. Reproduced with his kind permission.

The Belfast auction houses

I contacted the main Belfast auction houses which had been in business in 1949 to discover if they had any record of the sale, but they had all lost their archives in bombings in the 1970s. I then searched all the weekly auction notices that appeared on the front page of *The Belfast Newsletter* (the oldest English language daily newspaper in the world still publishing today) for the six months before Robin Walsh's wedding in April 1949. Many

20 News Letter, Friday, August 27, 2010
20 Feature
www.newsletter.co.uk

Ballycastle piano strikes chords with the past

THE ROAMER

AN unusual story about a piano arrived in my in-tray this week. The instrument has strong connections with Northern Ireland, a story peppered with wonderful coincidences, and a few unanswered questions.

Michael Hannon, former director of Sheffield University Library, contacted me about his Broadwood Square Piano, purchased by his late mother, Mrs Hilda Hannon, in P J McIlroy's auction rooms in Ballycastle in 1977.

The piano was built in 1804 and Michael eventually had it professionally restored in the early 1980s.

"It still plays well," he told me. He's trying to trace its full history, and hopes we can help. Late last year Mr Hannon discovered that a large

Wilson.

"We have also discovered that Mrs Findlay's new granddaughter was christened on August 10," added Michael, "so we assume that having waited for the child's safe arrival and christening she sailed back to Glasgow with her new piano."

Mrs Findlay was the widow of wealthy tobacco merchant, Robert Findlay, who had made his fortune in Virginia and bought the splendid town house in Miller Street as well as a grand country house called Easterhill.

"We assume that the piano was first delivered to Miller Street before being delivered to Easterhill," reckons Michael, who's also traced a family link between Mrs Findlay and the current Robert Findlay 'the 8th of Boturich', who lives on the banks of Loch Lomond.

The piano's story now begins to unfold with great intrigue and co-incidence.

"To my astonishment," said Michael, "I read that one of Mrs Findlay's grandsons, Thomas Dunlop (known as T D), had gone into business with a Peter Denny, a shipbuilder in

on a whim in Ballycastle had any family connection."

Mr Hannon contacted P J McIlroy's son Sean who now runs the business in Ballycastle, where his mother purchased the piano, and Sean well remembers helping his father carry the instrument into the auction.

He also remembers that the vendor of the piano was a Robin Walsh who lived in Cushendun, and still lives there, now aged 88.

"I contacted him," Michael told me, "and he sent me a photo of the piano which he bought at auction in Belfast in 1949 for, he thinks, £7 10 shillings, including a tip to the porter who did the bidding. He bought the piano to help furnish the flat in Belfast which he and his wife lived in just after they got married. Sadly he can't recall which auction room sold the piano."

So Michael now knows who originally owned the piano, and where it was in 1949, "but I need to know how and when it came to Ireland. I do know that Easterhill, the Findlay family house, was demolished in the 1930s, so if the piano was still there at that time, it may have been given to a

The Broadwood Square Piano's carved name

Opening the Broadwood Piano's lid on history

'Ballycastle Piano strikes chords with the past', article published 27th August 2010. Reproduced courtesy of The Belfast Newsletter.

pianos, including some Broadwoods, were listed but there was no specific mention of a Broadwood *square* piano or other keyboard instruments with which it might have been confused.

As I had made no progress with auction records, Robin Walsh suggested I contact 'The Roamer', a regular column in the *Newsletter*. This resulted in a half-page feature on 27th August 2010 entitled 'Ballycastle piano strikes chords with the past'.

The feature outlined the story so far and invited older readers to send in any pre-1949 memories they might have had of the piano in their homes when they were children, but no responses were forthcoming.

How did the piano reach Belfast?

This still left a gap of nearly a century and a half with no record of where the piano had been, so what might have happened to it and how did it reach Ireland? Among a host of possibilities, the following appear plausible:

a) *Dorothea Findlay*: when Robert the Banker sold the Findlay townhouse at 42 Miller Street in

1818, it seems likely that the piano, which was only 14 years old, would have been taken out to Easterhill where Dorothea, then aged 26 and still unmarried, was living with her brother Robert, his young family and their elderly mother. Still having piano lessons with John Donaldson, she would have preferred to continue using the same instrument, but when she married him in 1820 in the teeth of family opposition, she would have been encouraged to take the piano away with her. Had it remained at Easterhill, it would have had distressing 'Donaldson' connotations for her mother and brother. There was no mention of the piano in Donaldson's will but had it been among his possessions, it would probably have been included in his general furniture and, by then over 60 years old and heavily used, found its way into the second hand trade in Edinburgh and thence eventually to Ireland.

b) *Donaldson & McFeat:* it is possible that if the Findlays had *not* taken the piano out to Easterhill, they might have sold it through Donaldson's shop in Glassford Street which, in 1818, was still trading as a Broadwood agency. The shop would have resold it locally or into the trade beyond Glasgow, perhaps even to the Belfast Broadwood agent William Ware, as trading and social links between the two cities were very well established.

c) *William Ware of Belfast:* Ware, who was organist at St Anne's Parish Church in Belfast from 1786-1825, was also a Broadwood agent with a flourishing trade. As John Broadwood chose to send *him* some experimental examples of his early square pianos, he would already have established a name for himself among the network of Broadwood agents. Ware also had a better known assistant in Edward Bunting, whose *General Collection of Irish Music arranged for the Pianoforte*, was first published in 1796; as it had been so well received, Donaldson would have had copies of this popular work for sale in his shop in Glassford Street.

When Donaldson visited Dublin in 1815 to study Logier's teaching methods, it is possible that he also visited Belfast to meet Bunting, discuss Broadwood agency business with Ware and perhaps play the prestigious Snetzler organ that Ware had had installed in St Anne's Church in 1781. As Donaldson's father had been a pupil of John Snetzler, an organ builder of Swiss origin who worked mostly in England, he may even have played a part in its installation in Belfast. Had this meeting taken place, Donaldson and Ware could have agreed to cooperate in trading second-hand instruments the short distance across the Irish Sea; this was just three years before the square piano would have been removed from the Findlays' town house in Miller Street.

d) *A Scottish family moving to Ireland:* it is also possible that the piano crossed the Irish Sea with a Scottish family moving to Ireland on business, perhaps one with a shipbuilding connection such as William Denny II (b. 1815) who had worked as Chief Draughtsman for the Coats & Young yard in Belfast before returning home to become a founding partner in Denny Brothers in 1844.

Future research

These possibilities appear plausible to a greater or lesser degree but it seems unlikely that any new documentary or personal evidence will come to light to fill the gap of almost a century and a half. Mrs Findlay's Broadwood square piano must have many more intriguing tales to tell.

The piano now and in the years ahead

Mrs Findlay's piano is regularly tuned and maintained by Ken Sleaford in Sheffield. Because of its age and wooden frame, it is now tuned a minor 3rd below A440 cycles per second, what we know as 'concert pitch': this reduces the tension on the strings and the risk of the wooden frame warping. Inja Davidović's square piano recordings on the CD at the back of this book were made at this pitch.

Whatever bitter rifts the piano may have witnessed between the Findlay family and John Donaldson, it seems appropriate that it might find its final home in St Cecilia's Hall within Edinburgh University's Collection of Historic Musical Instruments, originally established by Donaldson around 1850 and not far from where he and his wife Dorothea lie buried. Before then I trust that it will be played and well looked after by at least one more generation of my own family.

Inside St Cecilia's Hall at Edinburgh University. Photo: EUCHMI.

Acknowledgements

I am indebted to Dr Alasdair Laurence, Chairman of John Broadwood & Sons Ltd, and to Robert Simonson, Curator of the Broadwood Archives in the Surrey History Centre, who provided the information from the Broadwood porters' books documenting Mrs Findlay's purchase of the square piano in 1804. Without their specialist help, this book could not have been written.

Similarly, the extraordinary connections between the Findlay and Denny families and the saga of 'The Flighty Dorothea' Findlay and John Donaldson would not have come to light if the late Robert Findlay, the 8th of Boturich, had not been interviewed for *Burke's Peerage and Gentry* in 2001 by Sarah Powell. It was through the interview transcript that I made first contact with Robert and Liisa Findlay, then with Robert's brother Bill and his wife Delia. I am indebted to all four of them for their help and generous hospitality. Succeeding his brother Robert as family historian, Bill Findlay introduced me to the wonderful Findlay 'Red Book'.

I'm indebted to Sean McIlroy who had helped his late father PJ McIlroy carry the square piano into their Ballycastle auction room in 1977 and, crucially, remembered that Robin Walsh was the vendor; I'm equally indebted to Robin Walsh for telling me about buying the piano in 1949 and sending me the photograph of it in his Belfast flat.

My brothers Leslie and David Hannon provided invaluable information about our grandfather Leslie Denny and our uncle Edward Denny. I am indebted to our cousin Robin Denny who very helpfully steered me away from several errors relating to the history of Dennys. My brother-in-law David Hume also gave me useful information about Leslie Denny's work on paddle wheel design and ship stability.

For the history of Broadwoods I have drawn extensively on two key books: David Wainwright's *Broadwood by Appointment - a History* (London: Quiller Press, 1982), covers its history from the earliest days; Michael Cole's excellent book

Broadwood Square Pianos (Cheltenham: Tatchley Books, 2005) took full advantage of the newly catalogued Broadwood Archives and is now the definitive work on the subject. I also thank Michael Cole for his expert advice via email.

I'm deeply indebted to Professor Sir Tom Devine for his book *The Tobacco Lords* (Edinburgh: Donald, 1975) and his chapter *The Golden Age of Tobacco in Glasgow, Volume 1: Beginnings to 1830* (Manchester: Manchester UP, 1995); I have drawn heavily on both books for information on the city's wealthy tobacco merchants.

My special thanks go to Professor Arnold Myers who showed me round the Edinburgh University Collection of Historical Musical Instruments (EUCHMI), originally established by John Donaldson, and to Dr Christopher Field who provided extensive source material and very helpful advice relating to John Donaldson and his organ-builder father. Their 'Calendar of John Donaldson's Life' on the EUCHMI website was a particularly useful source.

I thank Ian Whittaker for alerting me to the opening of the Forth & Clyde Canal in 1790 and Guthrie Hutton for advice on its early history and permission to reproduce images from his *Forth & Clyde Canalbum*. Alister McCrae and Alan Prentice's *Irrawaddy Flotilla* (Paisley: Paton, 1978) draws on their early experience working for the Irrawaddy Flotilla Company and gives a fascinating insight into the Findlay/Denny partnership.

Unable to trace their publisher or families for permission to reproduce illustrations, I would be grateful for their contact details.

I thank the following institutions and their staff: *The Belfast Newsletter,* particularly Charlie Warmington, writer of 'The Roamer' column; the British Library, particularly the Music and Maps Libraries, Imaging Services and Permissions Section; the Colt Clavier Collection for permission to reproduce the portrait of Thomas Broadwood; Dumbarton Library Heritage Centre, particularly Sam Moore and Isabel Paterson, for research services in the Findlay and Denny Archives; Edinburgh University's Fine Art Collection and the University Library Centre for Research Collections, for background material on John Donaldson.

I thank the Glasgow Building Preservation Trust for their help with the history of The Tobacco Merchant's House in Miller Street, the Scottish Civic Trust (now based there) for access to it, Jim Opfer and Russell Logan (of Opfer Logan Architects) who oversaw its restoration, and Joe Shaldon for his photograph of it; Glasgow University Library Hunterian Museum & Art Gallery, for photographic services and the University Archive Services for access to graduation records; the Kipling Society, specially their Honorary Librarian John Lambert, for photographs of Irrawaddy Flotilla vessels and pointing me to Kipling's *Song of the Banjo*; the Linenhall Library in Belfast for access to newspaper back runs; Lloyd's Register Historical Research

Service, especially Anne Crowne, for information on the sloop *Eliza*; and the London Topographical Society, particularly Mike Wicksteed and Roger Cline, for advice on London maps.

I thank the Met Office National Meteorological Archive for 1804 London weather reports; MOTCO Enterprises for the image of Fairburn's 1802 Map of London; the Mitchell Library in Glasgow, especially Patricia Grant, for help with photographic research; the Museum of the Mound, Edinburgh, specially Amanda Noble, for the image of the Glasgow & Ship Bank £1 note; the National Library of Scotland for images of Glasgow Postal Directories; the National Maritime Museum, Greenwich, for portrait and photographic research services; the National Oceanography Centre in Liverpool for 1804 Thames tide tables; the National Portrait Gallery for portrait images; the Royal Commission on the Ancient and Historical Monuments of Scotland for the aerial photograph of *Helenslee*; St Fagans National History Museum in Cardiff, particularly Dr Emma Lile, for photographs of Zumpe's early square pianos; the Scottish Maritime Museum, especially Linda Ross, for photographic research, and staff at the Denny Ship Model Experimental Tank; Sheffield University Library, particularly Jacky Hodgson, Elaine Ashton and Val Harding, for sourcing maps and digitization services; the State Library of Victoria's Green Collection, for the photograph of the *SS Rotomahana*; the Trades House of Glasgow, specially John Gilchrist, Clerk to the House, for the photograph of the Trades Hall; the V&A Museum for portrait images; and the Library of Virginia for the cartouche from the 1751 Map of Virginia.

Among digital records consulted for family details, the most important were: *Scotland's People*, the official Scottish genealogical resource; *FamilySearch*, the genealogical service provided by the Church of Jesus Christ of Latter Day Saints; Census Records; and The National Archives.

I also thank the following individuals for their invaluable help: the late Angela Green for background information on Rev Charles Bannatyne and his sister Dorothea; Dr Eric Kentley, author of the *Cutty Sark Souvenir Guide*, for information about Dennys' role in completing the ship; Professor Graham Lappin for photographs of the *SS Coya* on Lake Titicaca; Dr Peter Mole for his advice on early keyboard instruments; Dr Elaine Moohan of the Open University in Scotland for information on the Sacred Music Institution in Glasgow and the Donaldson 'Grand Organ'; Professor Michael Moss, previously of Glasgow University, for information on Peter Denny; Laura Peat for the photograph of Boturich Castle; Kate Pickering for her charming drawing of the square piano being delivered to New Broad Street; and Kirsty Prince for her photographs throughout the book. Any uncredited photographs I took myself.

I thank Roy Knowles who did such an excellent job restoring the square piano in 1979/80 and Ken Sleaford in Sheffield who keeps it in good playing order. My special thanks go to Inja Davidović for her superb recordings on the CD found at the end of this book, and Dr Adam Stansbie for his expertise in recording and producing it. I thank Dr Mary Dullea, Director of Performance in Sheffield University's Department of Music, for putting me in touch with Inja Davidović; also Professor Simon Keefe and the Department of Music for facilitating the Donaldson *Sonata* recording on the University's Steinway grand piano.

My special thanks go to my brother David Hannon and his wife Joan, and to Mark Pickering for their helpful comments on an early draft of the text. I am responsible for any historical, technical or other errors and would welcome comments where I may have gone astray.

I thank Emma Nunnington, Lee Hall, Christopher Holland, Mark Newbold and the team at Northend Creative Print Solutions in Sheffield for their enthusiasm and professional expertise with the design and publication of this book. I also thank Neelam Modi who illustrated the two family trees inside the front cover.

My warmest thanks go to my wife Rosemary, who has been my excellent research assistant, my most helpful critic and greatest support throughout the long gestation of this book. We have known Mrs Findlay's square piano since 1977 and trust that when it is eventually handed on to the next generation(s) of our family, it will remain in good hands.

Finally, I shall always be grateful to my mother, Hilda Hannon, for buying the square piano in 1977 and giving it to me: without it, there would have been no story to tell.

Michael Hannon
Sheffield, 2015

Inja Davidović writes:

Playing the Broadwood square piano

When we first discussed the CD accompanying this book, our intention was that I should record the Donaldson Sonata on the Broadwood square piano but, following a short rehearsal, it became clear that this would not be possible. Although after some 200 years the piano is in very good condition, it was highly demanding to play because, over time, it has developed its own personality: the odd key remains depressed, the pedal occasionally squeaks, and the hammers in the upper register are overly percussive. However, there was a much more significant challenge: the tuning has been lowered by a minor third to reduce stress on the wooden frame, and this creates a rather unexpected colouration when played.

A range of pieces was trialled, but changes in colour and dynamics were often too extreme. To accompany this book, it seemed appropriate that the piano should dictate the nature of pieces selected for the CD. The three movements from the Bach English Suites particularly suited the percussive nature of the piano. By contrast, Field's Nocturne No.5 in B-flat Major seemed appropriate for its unique colouration, allowing for a slow-paced piece to be included. The Broadwood has clearly aged, and its character has presumably changed. Even so, through these recordings, one might imagine how this wonderful instrument, a product of a remarkable and transitional point in the musical landscape of the British Isles, would have sounded over 200 years ago.

Recording John Donaldson's 'Sonata for the Piano Forte in G Minor'

Published around 1822, Donaldson's large-scale Sonata represented a very different pianistic challenge. To give it the performance it deserves, we agreed that I should record it on a modern Steinway Grand. In addition to the highly progressive harmonies, the piece straddles both classical and romantic styles, thus exemplifying some of the adventurous and advanced compositional interests often associated with the London Pianoforte School. Donaldson's musical influences are present throughout. However, his highly developed compositional voice and rigorous attention to detail, give the work a unique style and character.

The longest movement, *Allegro Moderato, Ma Molto Energetico,* is both majestic and vibrant. Two themes, developed throughout the movement, begin with the august and splendid before bursting into a series of energetic and elaborate variations. In *Adagio, Con Espressione e Molto Legato,* Donaldson's Schubertian adagio further develops motifs from the previous movement; the substantially slower tempo, alongside the re-contextualisation of melodic materials, demonstrates the versatility of Donaldson's